STEPHEN JOSEPH SCOTT examines history through a historical materialist class-oriented lens, focus, and analysis. He has been published in an array of publications, such as *The Black Agenda Report, The Hampton Institute, Toward Freedom, Dissident Voice, Midwestern Marx, Sublation Magazine, CineAction, Counter-Currents, and The Bullet.*

He completed all of his Post Graduate Master's Studies in History at The University of Edinburgh Scotland; and, is an alumnus, essayist, and author associated with the School of History, Classics & Archeology - Earning a Master's level Post Graduate Degree in the Science of History with Merit from The University of Edinburgh's MSc Program in History 2024.

Stephen graduated Summa Cum Laude with a B.A. in History from the College of Social and Behavioral Sciences at the University of Arizona. He is also a singer/songwriter, humanist/activist – a self-taught musician, performer, and actor. As a musician, he uses American Roots Music to illustrate the current social and political landscape. He currently lives in Mount Airy, Philadelphia.

CLASS DISTINCTIONS

THRU
HISTORY IN REVIEW

A Collection of Essays by Stephen Joseph Scott

First published by Gael Publishing 2024
Philadelphia, PA 19119

ISBN-13: 9798302211927

CONTENTS

Published Work
Ch. 1: *Martin Luther King Jr. and the Socialist Within*   *1*
✓   Hampton Institute   01/26/2021
✓   Black Agenda Report   01/27/2021
Ch. 2: *The Myth of American Exceptionalism*   *15*
✓   Toward Freedom   09/20/2021
Ch. 3: *The Moment King Was Slain*   *20*
✓   Dissident Voice   04/04/2022
Ch. 4: *Between Crosshairs a Man and His Revolution*   *25*
✓   Hampton Institute   04/13/2022
✓   Dissident Voice   04/17/2022
✓   Midwestern Marx   07/07/2023
Ch. 5: *Better Red Than Dead*   *41*
✓   Sublation Magazine   11/11/2022
Ch. 6: *What Hollywood Communicates Through the Movie Green Book: Race, Ethnicity, National Identity, Gender, Culture and Class in 1962 America*   *57*
✓   CineAction   04/24/2023
Ch. 7: *Ideology and Hypocrisy Amid Slavery and Democracy - Strange Bedfellows from Time Immemorial*   *72*
✓   Midwestern Marx   05/29/2023
✓   Hampton Institute   08/27/2023
Ch. 8: *Governance, Race, Property and Profit*   *88*
✓   The Bullet   02/27/2024
Ch. 9: *Where the Negroes Are Masters (A Book-Review)*   *100*
✓   Counter-Currents   03/18/2024

Unpublished Work
Ch. 10: *Philadelphia and the Darkside of Liberty: A Dissertation* *103*
     Introduction   *105*
     Ch. 1: The Paradox of Early American Freedom   *111*
     Ch. 2: Cui Bono – Who Benefitted Most from the Categorical Constructs of Race and Class?   *129*
     Ch. 3: The Atomization of the Powerless and the Sins of Democracy   *144*
     Conclusion   *161*
Bibliography   *165*
Index   *191*

Chapter One

MARTIN LUTHER KING JR. AND THE SOCIALIST WITHIN

To date, the image and memory of Martin Luther King Jr., social justice warrior, peace activist, and civil rights icon in the United States, and around the world, has been manipulated, watered-down, or diminished of meaning to serve the very forces of capitalist power and domination that the man spent his life in opposition to. In school textbooks in the U.S. for example, young people are taught about King the moderate man of peace, but not the radical King[1] who, criticized by other civil rights leaders for speaking out against the Vietnam War, proclaimed, on April 4, 1967 at Riverside Church in New York City, the U.S. to be, "the greatest purveyor of violence in the world today."[2] By sanitizing the image of the man, they, corporate and governmental powers, not only control the narrative, but they dumb down and oversimplify the message by lobotomizing the historical record. As W.E.B. Du Bois, American intellectual, asserted:

---

[1] Derrick P. Alridge, "The Limits of Master Narratives in History Textbooks: An Analysis of Representations of Martin Luther King, Jr.," *Teachers College Record* 108, no. 4 (April 2006): 673–680.

[2] Martin Luther King Jr., "Beyond Vietnam" (Speech, New York, NY, April 4, 1967), accessed November 5, 2020, The Martin Luther King Papers Project, Stanford University: https://kinginstitute.stanford.edu/king-papers/documents/beyond-vietnam.

"The difficulty, of course, with this philosophy is that history loses its value as an incentive and example: it paints perfect men and noble nations, but it does not tell the truth."[3] What Du Bois was saying is that by stripping, containing, and distorting historical narratives the learner is robbed of the substance, nuance, and otherness that history should provide. Each year in January as King is honored in the eyes of the public, there is little mention of the demands of the man and his mission: his fight for economic justice in a society that was built on inequality from the very start, "We can't have a system where some of the people live in superfluous, inordinate wealth while others live in abject, deadening poverty."[4] King the radical has been passed over and neutralized in order to make a moderate image of the man more digestible, not only to whitewash the general public and students alike but also to pacify the capitalist and white supremacist power structures that he so fiercely opposed.

In an early and intimate correspondence, written in 1952, to his then *jeune amour* Coretta Scott, King declared "I am more socialistic in my economic theory than capitalistic."[5] When addressing a book sent to him by Coretta: Edward Bellamy's *Looking Backward: 2000-1887,* King expressed: "On the negative side ... Bellamy falls victim to the same error that most writers of Utopian societies fall victim ... idealism

---

[3] W.E.B. Du Bois, quoted in Kevin Bruyneel, "The Martin Luther King Jr. Memorial and the Politics of Collective Memory," *History & Memory* Vol. 26 (April 2014): 75–108.

[4] Martin Luther King, Jr., quoted in Julian Bond, "Remember the Man and the Hero, Not Just Half the Dream," *Seattle Times*, April 3, 1993, accessed November 5, 2020, at https://projects.seattletimes.com/mlk/archives.html#bond.

[5] Martin Luther King Jr., "To Coretta Scott," July 18, 1952, accessed November 3, 2020, King Papers: https://kinginstitute.stanford.edu/king-papers/documents/coretta-scott.

not tempered with realism."[6] King was a pragmatist who understood fully the cause and effect of a capitalist system that pushed aside the needs of its populous in the name of profit, "So today capitalism has outlived its usefulness. It has brought about a system that takes necessities from the masses to give luxuries to the classes. So I think Bellamy is right in seeing the gradual decline of capitalism."[7] This letter reveals that King was an admitted Socialist and firm in his agreement with Bellamy's prediction of the inevitable degeneration of capitalism.

Reflecting upon his longtime hero and mentor, Norman Thomas, King espoused the 1932 Socialist Presidential nominee's views as an inspiration to his own antiwar stance concerning Vietnam in an article published in *Pageant* magazine in June 1965, "Thomas, a Presbyterian minister, found his interest in socialism stimulated by the antiwar declaration of the Socialist Party in 1917."[8] It was to President Franklin Roosevelt's acclaim, that he, once in office, took on much of Thomas' socialist platform when putting together his well-known New Deal program: "Old-age pensions for men and women 60 years old; Abolition of child labor; The six-hour day, five-day week with no wage reductions; Health insurance and maternity insurance; and, Adequate minimum wage laws."[9] King inspired by Thomas' unorthodox socialist approach to the issues of his day, steadfastly admired his principled stand calling him "The Bravest Man I've Ever Met," and embodied Thomas' following sentiments in words

---

[6] Ibid.

[7] Ibid.

[8] Martin Luther King Jr., "The Bravest Man I Ever Met," *Pageant*, June 1965, accessed November 6, 2020, at https://freepress.org/article/bravest-man-i-ever-met.

[9] Ibid.

and deeds, "The hope for the future lies in a new social and economic order which demands the abolition of the capitalist system."[10] The seeds were planted; the capitalist opponent and unyielding guardian of socialist values stood evident throughout King's ministry.

January 10 1957 marked the birthday of the Southern Christian Leadership Conference at Ebenezer Baptist Church in Atlanta, Georgia, founded by Martin Luther King Jr. and his father, to fight for civil rights and economic fairness. Increasingly throughout the 1960s, King became more anticorporate; and, more explicitly judgmental of capitalism as a system of innate inequality. In May 1967, while speaking at a SCLC staff meeting, King pushed radical against the injustices baked into the fundamental structure of capitalism, as well as the corrupt and unethical political system that allowed it to ride roughshod over its own population, "We must recognize that we can't solve our problem now until there is a radical redistribution of economic and political power."[11] Meaning, the movement had to demand a radical paradigm shift in the administrative and monetary structures that undergirded the American system of capitalism, "We must see now that the evils of racism, economic exploitation, and militarism are all tied together you cant [sic] really get rid of one without getting rid of the others the whole structure of American life must be changed."[12] Again, in August 1967, at a SCLC annual conference, King asked, "Why are there forty million poor people in America? ... When you begin to ask that question, you are raising questions about the economic

---

[10] Ibid.

[11] Martin Luther King Jr., "To Charter Our Course for the Future" (Speech, Frogmore, SC, May 22, 1967), accessed November 14, 2020, at https://kairoscenter.org/mlk-frogmore-staff-retreat-speech-anniversary/.

[12] Ibid.

system, about a broader distribution of wealth ... you begin to question the capitalistic economy."[13] King was insistent that the resistance to an unjust system of inequality had to arise. In fact, in that same speech, in defense of workers' rights, King invoked Walter Reuther, leader of organized labor, founder of the United Auto Workers of America, and civil rights activist, "Walter defined power one day. He said, power is the ability of a labor union like UAW to make the most powerful corporation in the world, General Motors, say 'Yes' when it wants to say 'No.' That's power."[14] King, the supporter of cooperative ethics, denoted unions and the ability of workers to bargain collectively against corporate supremacy as an essential tool in checkmating capital and its abuses.

As explained by historian Thomas Jackson, King was definitive as to where public policy in the U.S. needed to go, "Policy must 'reduce the gap' between the poor and the majority by making the poverty line a percentage of median income."[15] King argued, raising the poverty line, which was inordinately low in 1964,[16] would bring a response to millions of working poor that President Lyndon Johnson's War on Poverty overlooked. In King's estimation, the inadequacy of the government's solution to the War on Poverty coupled with the war in Vietnam equaled a travesty that disproportionately punished the disenfranchised:

---

[13] Martin Luther King Jr., "Where Do We Go From Here?" (Speech, Atlanta, GA, August 16, 1967), accessed November 6, 2020, King Papers: https://kinginstitute.stanford.edu/king-papers/documents/where-do-we-go-here-address-delivered-eleventh-annual-sclc-convention.

[14] Ibid.

[15] Thomas F. Jackson, *From Civil Rights to Human Rights: Martin Luther King, Jr., and the Struggle for Economic Justice* (University of Pennsylvania Press, 2007), 272.

[16] Ibid.

[T]he war was doing far more than devastating the hopes of the poor at home. It was sending their sons ... to die.... So we have been repeatedly faced with the cruel irony of watching Negro and white boys on TV screens as they kill and die together for a nation that has been unable to seat them together in the same schools ... I could not be silent in the face of such cruel manipulation of the poor.[17]

The war in Southeast Asia, in King's view, was not only a brutal attack on a distant and poor "third-world" country halfway around the globe, but a direct assault on America's poor and working-class populace. Again, what King was asserting was that race, war, and economics were inextricably woven within the fabric of the U.S. political economy.

A New York Times editorial, dated April 7, 1967, published just three days after King's powerful antiwar declaration above, encapsulated the prevailing counter-assessment of the time. By ignoring class altogether, the conservative view of the day was camouflaged by "temperance," insisting that the war in Vietnam and racial injustice in the United States had nothing to do with each other, "The moral issues in Vietnam are less clear-cut than he suggests; the political strategy of uniting the peace movement and the civil rights movement could very well be disastrous for both causes."[18] The point this editorial avoided was the enormous sums of public funds spent on the war, and their violent social and economic impact domestically, which King defined as wasteful and destructive, "I knew that America would never invest the necessary funds or energies in

---

[17] King, "Beyond Vietnam."

[18] "Dr. King's Error," *The New York Times*, Editorial, (NYC, April 7, 1967), accessed November 26, 2020, King Papers: https://kinginstitute.stanford.edu/sites/mlk/files/kingserror.pdf.

rehabilitation of its poor so long as adventures like Vietnam continued to draw men and skills and money."[19] In place of King's economic mandate, the editorial used an erroneous conflation designed to convince the reader that melding the anti-war movement with civil rights was more about coupling the issues of race and militarism rather than King's actual emphasis, economic justice.

King first announced his Poor People's Campaign (a multiracial non-violent crusade focused on jobs and dignity for the poor) at a staff retreat for the SCLC in November 1967. After having crisscrossed America building an alliance for his PPC, gathering support through a coalition of Blacks, farm workers, Native Americans, and poor Whites, King delivered a speech, on March 10, 1968, in NYC (just a month prior to his assassination), entitled "The Other America." King sermonized before a union, Local 1199, mostly comprised of African Americans, "If all of labor were to follow your example of mobilizing ... our nation would be much closer to a swift settlement of that immoral, unjust, and ill-considered war."[20] It was this kind of tutelage, this kind of unifying, enlisting, and organizing of King's multiracial army of the poor and working class, that threatened the establishment, i.e., government officials, corporate elites, and mainstream media. Furthermore, in that same speech, King challenged not just the establishment and its propaganda, but also those among his ranks that doubted the efficacy of his mission to end the war:

> I would yet have to live with the meaning of
> my commitment to the ministry of Jesus Christ. To

---

[19] King, "Beyond Vietnam."

[20] Martin Luther King Jr., "The Other America, Address at Local 1199" (NYC, March 10, 1968), in *The Radical King*, ed. Cornel West (Beacon Press, 2015), 235–236.

me the relationship of this ministry to the making of peace is so obvious that I sometimes marvel at those who ask me why I am speaking against the war.[21]

King, the theologian, in defense of his anti-war stance, harkened back to the teachings of the social gospel as his grounding – itself, a radical pacifist document; and, a passionate plea for the rights and dignity of the poor.

On a prior date, April 14, 1967, at Stanford University, King had given a different version of the same speech, one in which he invoked Frederick Douglass, abolitionist, author, and former slave. King publicly attacked the United States and its long vicious history of elite control, systematic racism and unjust class bigotry:

> This is why Frederick Douglas [sic] could say that emancipation for the Negro was freedom to hunger ... freedom without roofs to cover their heads. He went on to say that it was freedom without bread to eat, freedom without land to cultivate. It was freedom and famine at the same time.[22]

King's acknowledgment of Douglass helps to clarify his radical view of the long and inhumane historical narrative, which defined America. He was telling his audience that in a system founded on greed, white supremacy, and inequality, freedom was not "freedom" if one was Black or poor. Written from his cell years earlier, in 1963, in his now celebrated *Letter From a Birmingham Jail,* King penned, "We know through painful experience that freedom is never voluntarily

---

[21] Ibid.

[22] Martin Luther King Jr., "The Other America, Address at Stanford University," April 14, 1967, accessed November 6, 2020, at https://www.crmvet.org/docs/otheram.htm.

given by the oppressor; it must be demanded by the oppressor.["23] In a top-down system of cascading violence King, the shepherd, attempted to give voice to the voiceless and consciousness to the beleaguered masses.

When matching the inequities of the American economic system against other systems, in May 1965, while speaking before the Negro American Labor Council, King lauded the Scandinavian modus of democratic socialism and demanded a fair and just redistribution of America's affluence: "Call it democracy, or call it democratic socialism, but there must be a better distribution of wealth within this country for all God's children."[24] Again, years earlier, from his jail cell in Birmingham, King, the radical humanist, had elegiacally weaved together the socialist values of the collective within faith, race, and socioeconomic condition, "I am cognizant of the interrelatedness of all communities and states ... We are caught in an inescapable network of mutuality, tied in a single garment of destiny. Whatever affects one directly, affects all indirectly."[25] Additionally, public statements like, "I think black people and poor people must organize themselves ... we must mobilize our political and economic power,"[26] congealed King's position as a "Communist," as well as a dangerous man whose every move needed to be tracked. Even if one publicly condemned communism as King certainly did, as far back as his Atlanta sermon, given on

---

[23] Martin Luther King Jr., "Letter from a Birmingham Jail," April 16, 1963, accessed November 14, 2020, at https://www.africa.upenn.edu/Articles_Gen/Letter_Birmingham.html.

[24] Martin Luther King Jr., "To the Negro American Labor Council," May 1965, quoted in Jackson, *From Civil Rights to Human Rights*.

[25] King, "Letter from a Birmingham Jail."

[26] King, "The Other America, Address at Local 1199." 243.

September 8, 1953, asserting, "Let us begin by stating that communism and Christianity are at the bottom incompatible. One cannot be a true Christian and a true Communist simultaneously."[27] An open denunciation of communism of this sort mattered little to the foundations of power that were bitterly opposed to the rights and unification of Blacks, the poor, and the working class, "Perhaps the quintessential example of a target of state surveillance was Martin Luther King Jr. The surveillance of King was carried out with great intensity by the FBI, in concert with local police forces."[28] The powers of the State were now solidified and King was the target of that solidification, "[King was] subject to increasing scrutiny and harassment from the FBI, which had wiretapped his phones since 1963,"[29] however, it did not begin under the Kennedy and Johnson administrations; it began much earlier, as early as the first freedom marches in Montgomery Alabama in the mid-1950s.

The FBI directive, dated January 4, 1956, is proof positive that the U.S. government was purposefully investing manpower and resources into tracking King as early as 1955: "On 7 December [1955], the FBI's Mobile Office began forwarding information on the bus boycott to FBI director J

---

[27] Martin Luther King Jr., "Communism's Challenge to Christianity" (Sermon, Atlanta, GA, September 8, 1953), accessed November 15, 2020, King Papers: https://kinginstitute.stanford.edu/king-papers/documents/communisms-challenge-christianity.

[28] Jules Boykoff, "Surveillance, Spatial Compression, and Scale: The FBI and Martin Luther King Jr.," *Antipode* 39, no. 4 (September 2007): 733.

[29] Megan Hunt et al., "'He Was Shot Because America Will Not Give Up on Racism': Martin Luther King Jr. and the African American Civil Rights Movement in British Schools," *Journal of American Studies* (August 20, 2020): 15.

Edgar Hoover."[30] The document, although redacted, reveals that the FBI's Special Agent in Charge was working closely with a Montgomery Police Officer gathering, with intent, as much defamatory evidence as possible against King in order to take him and his non-violent call for social justice down.[31]

The security state not only tracked King's every movement, but it also harassed him for years using an array of methods from penetrating surveillance to psychological coercion. The foundations of power were deeply distressed by King's radical decrees, and, his non-violent movement of civil disobedience, "The FBI was so concerned about King's radicalism and potential for inciting a black revolution that it deemed his activities a threat to national security."[32] In fact, the FBI sadistically mocked, taunted and provoked King to commit suicide in an anonymous letter sent to him November 21, 1964 - just nineteen days prior to his acceptance of the Nobel Peace Prize in Norway:

---

[30] "FBI Special Agent in Charge, Mobile, to J. Edgar Hoover" (SAC, Mobile, January 4, 1956), accessed November 15, 2020, King Papers:
http://okra.stanford.edu/transcription/document_images/Vol03Scans/96_4-Jan-1956_FBI%20Special%20Agent%20in%20Charge.pdf.
[31] Ibid.
[32] Alridge, "The Limits of Master Narratives in History Textbooks," 670.

You are a colossal fraud and an evil, vicious one at that ... like all frauds your end is approaching ... your Nobel Prize (what a grim farce) and other awards will not save you ... It is all there on the record, your sexual orgies ... you are done ... there is only one thing for you to do ... and you know what it is.[33]

This FBI missive proves that the forces within the government were willing to stop at nothing to end, what they considered, an imminent threat to the status quo. In fact, by April 3, 1968, after returning to Memphis (one day prior to his assassination), King's hostility toward the U.S. political economy and its endemic inequalities grew into an overt attack on corporate America, "We are asking you tonight ... to go out and tell your neighbors not to buy Coca-Cola in Memphis ... Tell them not to buy–what is the other bread? Wonder Bread."[34] This direct challenge to the pecuniary interests of American business only intensified the image of King as a menace.

Governmental forces so loathed King the man and what he stood for, that they pursued the diminution of his persona for years after his murder in Memphis, Tennessee, "While the FBI did intensely track King through his death, it actually continued to besmirch his name even after he was

---

[33] Anonymous, "Suicide Letter," November 1964, accessed November 15, 2020, printed by the New York Times: https://www.nytimes.com/2014/11/16/magazine/what-an-uncensored-letter-to-mlk-reveals.html?_r=1&referrer=.

[34] Martin Luther King Jr., "I've Been to the Mountaintop" (Speech, Memphis, Tenn., April 3, 1968), accessed November 6, 2020, King Papers: https://kinginstitute.stanford.edu/king-papers/documents/ive-been-mountaintop-address-delivered-bishop-charles-mason-temple.

assassinated,"[35] but what authoritarian forces working on behalf of capitalist interests could not completely eviscerate they inevitably subsumed. During his speech on the creation of a national holiday for King - November 2, 1983, some fifteen years after King's brutal assassination, Ronald Reagan was one of the first conservatives to publically confiscate, misappropriate, and alter King's image to that of the "extraordinary" American, "In the fifties and sixties, one of the important crises we faced was racial discrimination. The man whose words and deeds in that crisis stirred our nation to the very depths of its soul was Dr. Martin Luther King, Jr."[36] In spite of the fact that Reagan, and most reactionaries in the U.S., long considered King a traitor, a communist subversive, and, an adversary to corporate and state power, Reagan used King's words not only to support conservative ideals and policies, but also for his own political gain.[37] Facing re-election in 1984 and waning poll numbers, "[Reagan and] his political advisers hoped for some positive effect among black and moderate white voters."[38] Reagan, in what can be considered a public relations coup, exalted King's words

---

[35] Boykoff, "Surveillance, Spatial Compression, and Scale," 733.

[36] Ronald Reagan, "The Creation of the Martin Luther King, Jr., National Holiday" (Washington, DC, November 2, 1983), accessed November 6, 2020, at https://millercenter.org/the-presidency/presidential-speeches/november-2-1983-speech-creation-martin-luther-king-jr-national.

[37] Denise M. Bostdorff and Steven R. Goldzwig, "History, Collective Memory, and the Appropriation of Martin Luther King, Jr.: Reagan's Rhetorical Legacy," *Presidential Studies Quarterly* 35, no. 4 (December 2005): 669.

[38] Francis X. Clines, "Reagan's Doubts on Dr. King Disclosed," *New York Times*, October 22, 1983, accessed November 25, 2020 , at https://search.proquest.com/docview/424807626?rfr_id=info%3Ax ri%2Fsid%3Aprimo.

through a histrionic burst of American exceptionalism, "All of God's children will be able to sing with new meaning ... land where my fathers died ... from every mountainside, let freedom ring,"[39] which, as performed before the nation, deliberately sanitized, ignored and diminished the purpose of King's mission which stood in direct opposition to the destructive forces of corporate greed.

Finally, what this conservative, and later neo-liberal, approach to King's views conveniently overlooked, whether in political thought or school textbooks, is King's class-oriented fight for justice. Throughout his brief life, King affirmed, in private and in public, his socialist beliefs – from his stance on race, war, and poverty, to his evaluation of the global political economy. What the foundations of power have attempted to subvert, at all costs, was King's clarion call for the unification of the poor, "There is amazing power in unity. Where there is true unity, every effort to disunite only serves to strengthen the unity."[40] Again, Martin Luther King Jr. was a Socialist and radical humanist at his core, a resolute teacher of the social gospel, a committed supporter of cooperative principles, and a firm champion of collectivist values. As a result of his commitment to those ethics, principles, and values - he, not only fell victim to the pernicious and menacing powers of the capitalist state, but he also steadfastly and resolutely sacrificed his own life.

---

[39] Reagan, "The Creation of the Martin Luther King, Jr., National Holiday."

[40] Martin Luther King Jr., "The Violence of Desperate Men (1958)," in *The Radical King*, ed. Cornel West (Beacon Press, 2015), 20.

Chapter Two
THE MYTH OF AMERICAN EXCEPTIONALISM: FROM THE BEGINNING....

In his chapter entitled "Exceptionalism,"41 Daniel T. Rodgers argues that American exceptionalism is a historically contrived myth. Rodgers discusses the origins and evolution of the extant historicism that undergirds the embedded structural creed that says the United States stands alone as inimitable among nations. For example, Frederick Jackson Turner first struck an exceptionalist chord, in his 1893 essay, *The Frontier in American History,* with his "perennial rebirth" or "rebaptized as an American"[42] theme that proclaimed a singular American character through a rejection of the European ethos replaced by a unique pioneering spirit exclusive to "the American." Within a detailed examination of the dialectical shifts of American historiography, philosophy, and religion that pulsed through the American experience; from its earliest origins of the pious fundamentalism of the Massachusetts Bay Colony to the American Revolution; World War II; the Cold War and its current role as a global hegemonic superpower, Rodgers

---

[41] Daniel T. Rodgers, "Exceptionalism," in *Imagined Histories: American Historians Interpret the Past*, ed. Anthony Molho and Gordon S. Wood (Princeton, N.J: Princeton University Press, 1998), 21–40.

[42] Ibid., 25.

demystifies and untangles the "skein of tropes"[43] that underpin the "newness" and "distinctiveness" that defines America's historical, social and political "uniqueness."[44] Rodgers ignites his chapter with a question: Is America different? Then, through the use of scholarly and authoritative evidence, he methodically proceeds to lay bare the mythological foundations which buttressed America's fabled history - analyzing and exposing an unexceptional exceptionalism at its core for all to see. Yet, in spite of his, and other scholars' well-researched conclusions, Rodgers ends his chapter by exposing the persistent and entrenched depths of the American exceptionalist archetype, "Michael McGerr and Michael Kammen demonstrate [that within modern American historicism] challenges to the exceptionalist paradigm [still] generate sharp, visceral reactions."[45]

Rodgers, unswayed by post-1950s acculturation, looks back through time critically scouring the metahistorical chronicle in search of the decisive epochs that contributed most to the phenomenon called American "exceptionalism." His contribution is considered a seminal work in contemporary and post-exceptionalist historiography. Donald Pease writes, "Daniel T. Rodgers, perhaps the most articulate of a growing cadre of post-exceptionalist U.S. historians, has formulated the rationale for this collective endeavor with eminent clarity."[46] In his chapter, Rodgers proclaims that

---

[43] Ibid., 22.

[44] Ibid.

[45] Ibid., 35.

[46] Donald Pease, "American Studies after American Exceptionalism?" in *Globalizing American Studies* (University of Chicago Press, 2010), at https://chicago-universitypressscholarship-com.ezproxy.is.ed.ac.uk/view/10.7208/chicago/9780226185088.001.0001/upso-9780226185064-chapter-2

America's build-up and victory in WWII; its rise to global supremacy, and its dominance throughout the Cold War are central to decoding the portent of American exceptionalism. Contemporary scholars concur, "I agree that World War II set up an important phase in the history of American exceptionalism,"[47] states Ian Tyrell. Rodgers and his post-exceptionalist colleagues (through primary and secondary source material) expose past and present historiography by turning it on its head: Laurence Veysey points out, "it is clear that earlier interpretations of American history and culture, aggressively put forth as recently as the 1950s and emphasizing 'uniquely' American experiences and habits of mind, served largely to mislead us."[48] Eric Rauchway pushes even further by stating, "The concept of American exceptionalism does not really have anything to do with actual history,"[49] meaning that, in-depth analysis of the historical record reveals quite a different story.

Rodgers points to another specious characteristic of exceptionalist historicism; that being, the claim that providential intervention and America's cultural preeminence are guided, if not driven, by God, which defines the nation's "difference." Rodgers explains, "…difference in American national culture has meant "better": the superiority of the American way,"[50]and argues how unexceptional America is in this regard, "pride and providentialism are too widely spread to imagine them American peculiarities."[51] According

---

[47] Ian Tyrrell and Eric Rauchway, "The Debate Table: Eric Rauchway and Ian Tyrrell Discuss American Exceptionalism," *Modern American History* 1 (2018): 247–256.

[48] Laurence Veysey, "The Autonomy of American History Reconsidered," *American Quarterly* 31, no. 4 (1979): 455.

[49] Tyrrell and Rauchway, "Debate Table."

[50] Rodgers, "Exceptionalism," 22.

[51] Ibid.

to Rodgers, the dissemination of American exceptionalism, in the mid-20th century, was undergirded by a political, philosophical and psychological propaganda campaign: a deep rivalry with the USSR that led the United States to co-opt, and invert, a Stalinist neologism of the 1920s (i.e., Soviet "exceptionalism") and plant it firmly and inextricably, in its "divine" and rightful place: The United States of America! Yet, he queries even further, "what was the historiographical past of that conceit?"[52]

Rodgers traces the historiography back to an eighteenth-century travel writer, J. Hector St. John de Crévecoeur, who first described the Europeans [i.e., White males] inhabiting North America as unique and distinctive. Crévecoeur posed an essentialist question, "What Is an American?"[53] Rodgers demonstrates that Crévecoeur was, "Virtually unread in the United States before the twentieth century [his] lyric passage on ... [the] 'melting' of persons of all [European] nations into 'a new race of men' [was] extracted from context ... which now seemed to appear everywhere," co-opted and retitled, "What Is the American, This New Man?" by "Arthur Schlesinger, Sr., [American Historian who] made it the motif of his presidential address to the American Historical Association in 1942."[54] Rodgers asserts, "The literature of the new American Studies movement [from then on] was saturated with Crévecoeur references."[55] He continues, "They led off that catalyst of revisionist histories ... [including] Robert E. Brown's *Middle-Class Democracy and the Revolution in Massachusetts*, in 1955."[56] The United States was considered from that point on, in and out of the academy,

---

[52] Ibid., 21.
[53] Ibid., 37.
[54] Ibid., 27.
[55] Ibid.
[56] Ibid.

a uniquely singular phenomenon in world history. Rodgers exposes an irony, "…in their anti-Marxism, they reimagined Marx's general laws of historical motion applied everywhere but to their own national case."[57] Meaning, "John Winthrop's 'city upon a hill' … was no longer a mid-Atlantic hope … it was now America itself."[58] The exceptionality of American history was permanently fixed throughout the latter part of the 20th century until valiant and astute post-exceptionalists like Daniel T. Rodgers, and their counter-movement in American historiography, began to take hold.

---

[57] Ibid., 29.
[58] Ibid., 27.

Chapter Three

THE MOMENT KING WAS SLAIN:
How Opposition to Capital and Unification of the Poor Sealed His Fate

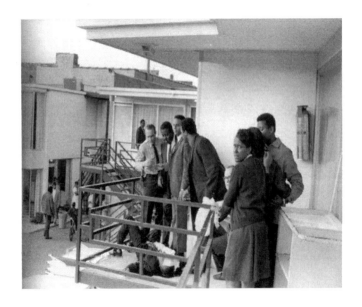

Source: Getty Images,
https://www.gettyimages.com/detail/news-photo/police-stand-with-civil-rights-leaders-ralph-abernathy-news-photo/2864527?adppopup=true

Dr. Martin Luther King Jr., civil rights legend and leader of the Southern Christian Leadership Conference, is murdered, the evening of April 4th, 1968 at 6:01 pm by an assassin's bullet outside his room, #306, on the 2nd-floor balcony of the Lorrain Motel in Memphis Tennessee.[59] This brutal act shocks the conscience of the nation and the world. If a picture is worth a thousand words, this photo by Joseph Louw, the only photographer on the scene that day, was taken just minutes after the infamous shot rang loud.[60]

King's body lies in a puddle of blood caused by a single-kill shot to the head, which struck him on the right side of his face splintering his jawbone and severing his carotid artery. Reverend Ralph Abernathy, Vice President at Large for the SCLC, and close friend of King, is standing to the right of a Memphis police officer, having just placed white cloths over King's wounds in a futile attempt to slow the bleeding. Abernathy is flanked by a panicked group of concerned associates and staff members including the renowned Rev. Andrew Young, Executive V.P. of the SCLC; and, Jesse Jackson. The young woman in the photo is turned back toward Louw with an expression of shock, fear, and bewilderment, which encapsulates the horrors of this historic moment frozen in time.

In March 1968, after months of traveling the country gathering support for his Poor People's Campaign, MLK arrived at the behest of his friend and fellow civil rights activist, Rev. James Morris Lawson, pastor of The Centenary United Methodist Church, in Memphis Tennessee.[61] King then leaves Memphis to address the concerns of poor people in Mississippi. By this point, MLK had dedicated years of his life to the struggle for civil rights in the United States: From

---

[59] Kent, *Free at Last.*

[60] Ibid.

[61] Stanford University, "Lawson, James M.," The Martin Luther King, Jr., Research and Education Institute, May 10, 2017, https://kinginstitute.stanford.edu/encyclopedia/lawson-james-m.

the 1956 marches in Montgomery Alabama to desegregate city buses; to the 1965 marches in Selma for the right to vote.[62]

On April 3[rd,] the day before his murder, King returned to Memphis to deliver the now famous *I've Been To The Mountain Top* speech, arguably one of the most profound and prophetic sermons of his life. In the speech, King seemingly prophesizes his own death: "Like anybody, I would like to live a long life. Longevity has its place. But I'm not concerned with that now."[63] King had spent months of exhaustive travel, crisscrossing America, fighting for the rights and dignity of poor people of all colors.[64] This issue, the defense of the poor and their dignity, has always been problematic: the unification of the poor and demands for social justice have historically stood as a threat to the establishment in the United States.

MLK and his movement of non-violent civil disobedience had come to symbolize that very threat. In fact, the movement demanded that Pres. Lyndon Baines Johnson ended the Vietnam War and used the money domestically, by giving it to those that needed it the most: America's poor.[65] MLK quickly becomes, in the eyes of America's power elite, i.e., government officials and American business interests, a very dangerous man. In 1964, LBJ, under pressure from MLK and his movement, ended segregation with the Civil Rights

---

[62] Martin Luther King Jr., "Martin Luther King, Jr.: All Labor Has Dignity," Truthout, January 19, 2015, https://truthout.org/articles/martin-luther-king-jr-all-labor-has-dignity/.

[63] Martin Luther King Jr., "'I've Been to the Mountain Top' (1968)," Oxford African American Studies Center, September 30, 2009, https://oxfordaasc.com/view/10.1093/acref/9780195301731.001.00 01/acref-9780195301731-e-33654.

[64] Martin Luther King Jr., "The Other America," Civil Rights Movement Archive, accessed October 15, 2020, https://www.crmvet.org/docs/otheram.htm.

[65] Kent, *Free at Last*.

Act and instituted a Voting Rights Act in 1965. That said, under both the Kennedy and Johnson administrations, J. Edgar Hoover's FBI tracked King's every movement for years, up until the moment of his death.[66]

By the time King delivered his address in Memphis, on March 18th, at the Bishop Charles Mason Temple, more than a thousand Negro sanitation workers walk off the job – after being savagely underpaid, brutally mistreated, and forced to work in filthy conditions. To a rousing crowd, MLK calls for a general work stoppage using non-violent civil disobedience. King states: "Don't go back on the job until the demands are met."[67] On March 28th, Memphis sanitation workers strike and thousands march alongside them bearing the slogan: "I Am A Man!" After The National Guard is brought in, and brutal and aggressive tactics by police are unleashed on demonstrators, Mayor Henry Loeb dismisses the workers' demands and refuses to recognize their union.[68] Fifty-seven days after the strike began; Loeb is finally willing to talk. On April 16th, just weeks after King's murder, the workers' demands are ultimately met.

This photo of MLK dead on the ground represents the loss of one of the greatest proponents of human rights in world history - not only for his people, but for all people of

---

[66] Stanford University, "Federal Bureau of Investigation (FBI)," The Martin Luther King, Jr., Research and Education Institute, May 2, 2017, https://kinginstitute.stanford.edu/encyclopedia/federal-bureau-investigation-fbi.

[67] King, "All Labor Has Dignity."

[68] DeNeen L. Brown, "'I Am a Man': The Ugly Memphis Sanitation Workers' Strike That Led to MLK's Assassination," *Washington Post*, February 12, 2018, https://www.washingtonpost.com/news/retropolis/wp/2018/02/12/i-am-a-man-the-1968-memphis-sanitation-workers-strike-that-led-to-mlks-assassination/.

conscience. The SCLC was like an aggrieved family that had lost its father. Rev. Ralph Abernathy poignantly states: "I'm not concerned with who killed MLK, I'm concerned with what killed MLK,"[69] referring to America's long and brutal history of violence and racism. On April 8th 1968, a symbolic march took place in Memphis, a profound gathering of resilience, homage to King's life and struggle, led by his widow Coretta Scott King and their children. That struggle continues today.

---

[69] BBC4, *Martin Luther King: The Assassination Tapes*, Documentary, 2018, https://learningonscreen.ac.uk/ondemand/index.php/prog/059FE7A 2?bcast=126443606.

Chapter Four

BETWEEN CROSSHAIRS, A MAN, AND HIS REVOLUTION

Imperial proprietorship over the small Caribbean Island of Cuba, from the United States' perspective, has been from its earliest founding understood as a foredrawn conclusion, a predetermined inexorable; a geographical inevitable. Heads of State, from Thomas Jefferson to James Monroe to John Quincy Adams et al. shared a similar conviction, "[that Cuba's] proximity did indeed seem to suggest destiny, a destiny unanimously assumed to be manifest."[70] Through the mid-19th century, US opinion toward Cuba was made jingoistically evident by Secretary of State John Clayton, "This Government," he advised, "is resolutely determined that the island of Cuba, shall never be ceded by Spain to any other power than the United States."[71] The Secretary went on to define his nation's hardened and inalterable commitment to the possession of the island, "The news of the cession of Cuba to any foreign power would, in the United States, be the instant signal for war."[72] These assertions were now foundational, as reiterated by Indiana Senator (and historian)

---

[70] Louis A. Pérez, "Between Meanings and Memories of 1898," *Orbis* 42, no. 4 (September 1, 1998): 501.

[71] William R. Manning, *Diplomatic Correspondence of the United States: Inter-American Affairs, 1831-1860* (Washington, 1932), 70.

[72] Ibid.

Albert J. Beveridge in 1901, "Cuba '[is] an object of transcendent importance to the political and commercial interests of our Union' and '[is] indispensable to the continuance and integrity of the Union itself,'"[73] sentiments that were (later) codified into the Cuban Constitution by the US (after the Spanish/American War of 1898) in the form of the Platt Amendment[74] ratified in 1903. Which Louis A. Perez soberly describes as, "[An] Amendment [that] deprived the [Cuban] republic of the essential properties of sovereignty while preserving its appearance, permitting self-government but precluding self-determination,"[75] in contradiction to (Cuba's heroic bard of national emancipation) José Martí's 19th-century grand vision of a truly liberated and self-governing island nation. In fact, this historic outlook permeated US strategy toward Cuba for the next century; merged in a complex web of amicable approbation combined with antagonistic condemnation, defiance, resentment, and ruin - all converging at a flashpoint called the Cuban Revolution of 1959, which not only shocked and bewildered US policymakers, but, for the first time, challenged their historic preconceptions of US hegemonic (i.e., imperial hemispheric) dominance. One man stood at the center of their bewilderment, criticism, disdain, and resentment: Fidel Alejandro Castro Ruz. Thus, US policy then directed at Cuba, by the early 1960s, was designed to punish this man, the small island nation, and its people, for his disobedience and defiance; and, as such, was intentionally aimed at destabilizing all efforts of rapprochement, as long as he (Castro) remained alive.

---

[73] Albert J. Beveridge, "Cuba and Congress," *The North American Review* 172, no. 533 (1901): 536.

[74] *The Platt Amendment*, May 22, 1903.

[75] Pérez, "Meanings and Memories," 513.

Although US intelligence (throughout the 1950s) provided the Eisenhower administration with a thorough history delineating the dangers of instability looming throughout the island, commanded by then military despot and "strong-man" Fulgencio Batista (who seized his return to power in an army coup in 1952), the US foolishly continued to provide economic, logistical and materiel support to the unpopular and graft-driven dictatorship.[76] US intelligence understood the potential danger posed by "[this] young reformist leader"[77] Fidel Castro and his band of revolutionaries. Castro and the 26th of July movement were a defiant response to what they considered a foreign-controlled reactionary government.[78] This response stood as a direct threat to the natural order of things, i.e., the US's historic prohibition (beyond legalistic euphemisms and platitudes)[79] of any genuine vestige of national sovereignty and self-determination by the Cuban people - which undergirded a belief that, like most Latin American states, the Cuban people were innately "child-like," incapable of true self-governance.[80] Beyond that, after the ousting of Batista, and "flush with victory," a young Fidel Castro, on January 2, 1959 (in Santiago de Cuba), assertively threw down the gauntlet, "this time, fortunately for Cuba, the revolution will not be thwarted. It won't be as in 1895 when the Americans came in at the last hour 'and made themselves masters of the

---

[76] Allen Dulles, *Political Stability In Central America and The Caribbean Through 1958* (CIA: FOIA Reading Room, April 23, 1957), 4–5.

[77] Ibid., 4.

[78] Fidel Castro, "History Will Absolve Me," 1953.

[79] *The Platt Amendment.*

[80] Lars Schoultz, *That Infernal Little Cuban Republic: The United States and the Cuban Revolution* (Chapel Hill, 2009), 58.

country.'"[81] Hence, as Jeffery J. Safford makes evident, this existential risk, in the minds of US policymakers, would have to be dealt with, embraced, evaluated, and analyzed (at least initially)[82] in order to maintain the desired outcome – i.e., evading Communist influence and maintaining economic "stability" through the protection of US interests on the island of Cuba no matter the cost.

In March of 1960, while naively underestimating Castro's success and support on the island, "the Eisenhower administration secretly made a formal decision to re-conquer Cuba … with a proviso: it had to be done in such a way that the US hand would not be evident."[83] Ultimately, US policymakers wanted to avoid a broader "backlash of instability" throughout the hemisphere by overtly invading the small island nation. That said, Castro and his revolutionaries understood the stark realities and nefarious possibilities cast over them, given the US's history of flagrant regime change throughout the region. Castro's accusations as presented at the United Nations, on 26 September 1960, which declared that US leaders were (intending if not) preparing to invade Cuba, were dismissed by the *New York Times* as "shrill with … anti-American propaganda."[84] Furthermore, Castro was ridiculed, by US representative James J. Wadsworth, as having "Alice in Wonderland fantasies"[85] of an invasion. But Castro's committed revolutionary coterie knew better, "In Guatemala in 1954 [Ernesto 'Che' Guevara witnessed] the first U.S. Cold War intervention [in the region] as U.S.-trained and backed

---

[81] Pérez, "Meanings and Memories," 514.

[82] Jeffrey J. Safford, "The Nixon-Castro Meeting of 19 April 1959," *Diplomatic History* 4, no. 4 (1980): 425–431.

[83] Noam Chomsky, *Rogue States: The Rule of Force in World Affairs* (London, 2000), 89.

[84] "Cuba vs. U.S.," *New York Times (1923-)*, January 8, 1961, 1.

[85] Ibid.

counter-revolutionary forces overthrew the democratically elected government of Jacobo Arbenz…"[86] In fact, similarly, the imminent Central Intelligence Agency (CIA) orchestrated assault, known as the Bay of Pigs (BOPs) invasion, under the Kennedy administration in April 1961, was heavily reliant upon anti-revolutionary factions, the Cuban people, and the military, rising up to join the invaders[87] – which as history proves, and journalist/author David Talbot underscores, did not come to pass:

To avoid Arbenz's fate, Castro and Guevara would do everything he had not: put the hard-core thugs of the old regime up against a wall, run the CIA's agents out of the country, purge the armed forces, and mobilize the Cuban people … Fidel and Che became an audacious threat to the American empire. They represented the most dangerous revolutionary idea of all – the one that refused to be crushed.[88]

This became an epic ideological battle in the myopic mind of US officials: the possible proliferation of an assortment of "despotic" Communist-controlled fiefdoms vs. the free world! Indeed, Arthur Schlesinger, Jr., special aide and historian to President John F. Kennedy in 1961-63, ominously warned the Executive, that "the spread of the Castro idea of taking matters into one's own hands,"[89] had great appeal in Cuba (and throughout Latin America), i.e.,

---

[86] Aviva Chomsky, *A History of the Cuban Revolution* (Chichester, West Sussex, U.K. ; Malden, MA, 2011), 98.

[87] "Official Inside Story Of the Cuba Invasion," *U.S. News & World Report*, August 13, 1979.

[88] David Talbot, *The Devil's Chessboard: Allen Dulles, the CIA, and the Rise of America's Secret Government* (New York, 2016), 338.

[89] "7. Memorandum From the President's Special Assistant (Schlesinger) to President Kennedy," in *Foreign Relations of the United States*, 1961-1963.

everywhere that, "distribution of land and other forms of national wealth greatly favor[ed] the propertied classes ... [thus] the poor and underprivileged, stimulated by the example of the Cuban revolution, [were] now demanding opportunities for a decent living."[90] This was the urgent and fundamental threat (or challenge) Fidel Castro and his movement posed to US hemispheric rule.

US media focused heavily on the plight of the "majority middle-class" Cuban exiles, that chose to leave the island as a result of the revolution's redistributive policies.[91] Cubans, particularly the initial waves, were dispossessed of substantial wealth and position and often arrived Stateside in chiefly worse conditions.[92] But *the essential question* as to, "why the [majority of] Cuban people [stood] by the Castro 'dictatorship'?,"[93] as Michael Parenti contends, was ignored by public officials and the press alike:

Not a word appeared in the U.S. press about the advances made by ordinary Cubans under the Revolution, the millions who for the first time had access to education, literacy, medical care, decent housing [and] jobs ... offering a better life than the free-market misery endured under the U.S.-Batista ancient régime.[94]

Castro's revolutionary ideals based on José Martí's patriotic theme of national sovereignty and self-determination effectively armed the Cuban people through a stratagem of

---

[90] "15. Summary Guidelines Paper: United States Policy Toward Latin America," in *FRUS*, 1961–1963.

[91] "Cuba: The Breaking Point," *Time*, January 13, 1961.

[92] Maria de los Angeles Torres, *In the Land of Mirrors: Cuban Exile Politics in the United States* (Ann Arbor, 2001), 75.

[93] Michael Parenti, "Aggression and Propaganda against Cuba," in *Superpower Principles U.S. Terrorism against Cuba*, ed. Salim Lamrani (Monroe, Maine, 2005), 70.

[94] Ibid.

socialist ideology and wealth redistribution meshed in a formula of land reform and social services (i.e., education, healthcare, jobs and housing) which included the nationalization of foreign-owned businesses; as such, US policymakers believed, "His continued presence within the hemispheric community as a dangerously effective exponent of 'Communism' and Anti-Americanism constitutes a real menace capable of eventually overthrowing the elected governments in any one or more 'weak' Latin American republics."[95] Fidel Castro was thus wantonly placed within the crosshairs of US covert action.

American officials assumed that the elimination of Castro was central to the suppression of his socialist principles, as Alan McPherson demonstrates, "In fall 1961, after the [BOPs] disaster, [JFK] gave the order to resume covert plans to get rid of Castro, if not explicitly to assassinate him."[96] Earlier in 1960, then CIA director, Allen Dulles' hardline that Castro was a devoted Communist and threat to US security "mirrored [those] of the business world such as William Pawley, the globetrotting millionaire entrepreneur whose major investments in Cuban sugar plantations and Havana's municipal transportation system were wiped out by Castro's revolution."[97] Thus, US officials, the Security State and US business interests were unified, "After Fidel rode into Havana on a tank in January 1959, Pawley [a capitalist scion] who was gripped by what Eisenhower called a 'pathological hatred for Castro,' even volunteered to pay for his assassination."[98] Countless attempts followed, thus, killing

---

[95] Philip Buchen, *Castro* (National Archives: JFK Assassination Collection, 1975), 4–5.

[96] Alan McPherson, "Cuba," in *A Companion to John F. Kennedy*, ed. Marc J. Selverstone (Hoboken, 2014), 235.

[97] Talbot, *The Devil's Chessboard*, 340.

[98] Ibid.

Castro became vital to the idea of US hemispheric "stability," i.e., capitalist economic and ideological control; and as such, Intelligence Services believed, "[The] political vulnerability of the regime lies in the person of Castro himself..."[99] Hence, the purging of Fidel Castro and the cessation of his ideas, through the punishment of the Cuban people, became not only the strategy of choice for the US, but its incessant authoritative doctrine. Accordingly, as longtime US diplomat to Cuba, Wayne Smith, verifies, the US's two overarching obsessive qualms which it believed required the eradication of Fidel Castro were: the long-term influence of his revolutionary socialist ideals in Latin America and beyond; and, the possible establishment of a successful Communist state on the island which would diminish US security, stature, image, influence and prestige in the hemisphere; and, in the eyes of the world.[100]

Through 1960-64, Castro had good reason to be on guard, "...the fact that the Kennedy administration was acutely embarrassed by the unmitigated defeat [at the BOPs] -indeed because of it- a campaign of smaller-scale attacks upon Cuba was initiated almost immediately."[101] Then Attorney General Robert F. Kennedy stated unequivocally, as Schlesinger reveals, that his goal, "was to bring the terrors of the Earth to Cuba."[102] RFK went on to emphasize the point that the eradication of the Castro "regime" was the US's central policy concern, "He informed the CIA that the Cuban

---

[99] Buchen, *Castro*, 7.

[100] Wayne S. Smith, "Shackled to the Past: The United States and Cuba," *Current History* 95 (1996).

[101] William Blum, *Killing Hope: US Military and CIA Interventions since World War II* (London, 2014), 186.

[102] Arthur M. Schlesinger Jr. quoted in Noam Chomsky and Marv Waterstone, *Consequences of Capitalism: Manufacturing Discontent and Resistance* (Chicago, 2021), 147.

problem carries, '...top priority in the United States Government -all else is secondary- no time, no effort, or manpower is to be spared.'"[103] Beyond the multifaceted covert actions directed at Cuba under Operation Mongoose, RFK and the US Joint Chiefs of Staff, aided by the CIA et al., implemented a long-term multi-pronged plan of punishment, focused on Cuba through Latin America, which included disinformation campaigns, subversion, and sabotage (they called hemispheric-defense-policies) that comprised a Military Assistance Program (MAP), which included economic support, subversive tactical training and materiel, devised to terminate "the threat" (i.e., Castro and his ideas) by establishing an Inter-American-Security-Force (of obedient states) under US control.[104]

With Cuba now in the crosshairs, in the early 1960s, "the CIA ... played savior to the [anti-Castro] émigrés, building a massive training station in Miami, known as JMWave, that became the agency's second largest after Langley, Virginia. In fact, it coordinated the training of what became known as the disastrous landing ... in 1961."[105] Conversely, historian Daniel A. Sjursen focuses more on JFK (than the CIA) as the culprit behind the heightened tensions amongst the three principal players. By 1962, with Cuba in the middle, both superpowers (the US and the USSR) stood at a standstill amid the very real possibility of a global conflagration which, Sjursen states, was primarily due to US bravado on behalf of a "military-obsessed" young President, "In preparing for a May 1961 summit meeting with Khrushchev [Kennedy

---

[103] Ibid.

[104] *The Joint Chiefs of Staff and Efforts to Contain Castro, 1960-64*, April 1981, 3, Learn.

[105] Alan McPherson, "Caribbean Taliban: Cuban American Terrorism in the 1970s," *Terrorism and Political Violence* 31, no. 2 (March 4, 2019): 393.

stated] 'I'll have to show him that we can be as though as he is....'"[106] Sjursen argues, "This flawed and simplistic thinking grounded just about every Kennedy decision in world affairs from 1961 to 1963 ... and would eventually bring the world to the brink of destruction with the Cuban Missile Crisis; and, suck the US military into a disastrous unwinnable war in Vietnam."[107] And yet, as Smith contends, Kennedy was certainly not without bravado, but ultimately, did make attempts to "defuse" the situation. Kennedy, Smith discloses, ruffled feathers within the Security State by, 1) his desire to end the Cold War, 2) his starting of a rapprochement with Castro (who was desirous of such - even if indirectly), and, 3) his goal to pull out of Vietnam.[108] In fact, with the Kennedy-Khrushchev negotiations finalized by JFK's promise not to invade Cuba if Soviet warheads were removed from the island – Khrushchev acquiesced, to Castro's dismay, but tensions did diminish.[109]

Be that as it may, Philip Brenner maintains, the crisis did not go away on 28 October 1962 for either the US or the USSR. The Kennedy-Khrushchev arrangements had to be implemented. On 20 November, the US Strategic Air Command was still on high alert: full readiness for war - with

---

[106] Daniel A. Sjursen, *A True History of the United States: Indigenous Genocide, Racialized Slavery, Hyper-Capitalism, Militarist Imperialism, and Other Overlooked Aspects of American Exceptionalism* (Lebanon, New Hampshire, 2021), 479.

[107] Ibid.

[108] Hampshire College TV, *2015 • Eqbal Ahmad Lecture • Louis Perez • Wayne Smith • Hampshire College*, 2016, accessed October 30, 2021, https://www.youtube.com/watch?v=IuBdKB8jX3I.

[109] Philip Brenner, "Kennedy and Khrushchev on Cuba: Two Stages, Three Parties," *Problems of Communism* 41, no. Special Issue (1992): 24–27.

the naval quarantine (i.e., blockade) firmly in place.[110] As a result, Castro stayed open to negotiations with the US, but at the same time purposefully cautious. "At this point, Castro, like Kennedy and Khrushchev, was circumventing his own more bellicose government in order to dialog with the enemy. Castro, too, was struggling, [but willing,] to transcend his Cold War ideology for the sake of peace. Like Kennedy and Khrushchev both, [he knew,] he had to walk softly."[111] Nevertheless, Castro stressed the fact that the Soviet Union had no right to negotiate with the US per inspections or the return of the bombers, "Instead, he announced, Cuba would be willing to comply based on [specific] demands: that the United States end the economic embargo; stop subversive activities ... cease violations of Cuban airspace; and, return Guantanamo Naval Base."[112] Of course, the United States security apparatus was arrogantly steadfast in its refusal to agree or even negotiate the matter.[113]

In spite of that, a rapprochement (devised by Kennedy diplomat, William Attwood, and, Castro representative to the UN Carlos Lechuga) surreptitiously endeavored through a liaison, journalist Jean Daniel of the *New Republic*, who stated that, Kennedy, retrospectively, criticized the pro-Batista policies of the fifties for "economic colonization, humiliation and exploitation" of the island and added that, "we shall have

---

[110] Philip Brenner, "Cuba and the Missile Crisis," *Journal of Latin American Studies* 22, no. 1 (1990): 133.

[111] James W. Douglass, *JFK and the Unspeakable: Why He Died and Why It Matters* (New York, 2010), 84.

[112] Brenner, "Cuba and the Missile Crisis," 133.

[113] "332. Letter From Acting Director of Central Intelligence Carter to the President's Special Assistant for National Security Affairs (Bundy)," in *FRUS*, 1961–1963.

to pay for those sins...."[114] Which may be considered one of the most brazenly honest statements, regarding the island, on behalf of an American President, in the long and complex history of US/Cuban relations. Daniel then wrote, "I could see plainly that John Kennedy had doubts [about the government's policies toward Cuba] and was seeking a way out."[115] In spite of JFK's pugnacious rhetoric directed at Cuba, during his 1960 Presidential campaign, Castro remained open and accommodating, he understood the forces arrayed upon the President, in fact, he saw Kennedy's position as an unenviable one:

I don't think a President of the United States is ever really free ... and I also believe he now understands the extent to which he has been misled.[116] ...I know that for Khrushchev, Kennedy is a man you can talk with....[117]

While in the middle of (an Attwood arranged and Kennedy sanctioned) clandestine meeting with Castro, Daniel reported, that (at 2 pm Cuban time) the news arrived that JFK was dead (shot in Dallas, Texas, on that very same day, 22 November 1963, at 12:30 pm), "Castro stood-up, looked at me [dismayed], and said 'Everything is going to change,...'"[118] and he was spot-on. Consequently, with (newly sworn-in) President Lyndon Baines Johnson mindful of the fact that Lee Harvey Oswald was "proclaimed" a Castro devotee, accommodations with the Cuban government would be much more difficult. As such, the Attwood-Lechuga connection was

---

[114] Jean Daniel, "Unofficial Envoy: An Historic Report from Two Capitals," *New Republic* 149, no. 24 (December 14, 1963): 15–20.

[115] Ibid.

[116] Ibid.

[117] Jean Daniel, "When Castro Heard the News," *New Republic* 149, no. 23 (December 7, 1963): 7–9.

[118] Ibid.

terminated.[119] Julian Borger, journalist for the *Guardian*, maintains that "Castro saw Kennedy's killing as a setback, [he] tried to restart a dialogue with the next administration, but LBJ was ... too concerned [with] appearing soft on communism,"[120] meaning opinion polls, and their consequences, trumped keeping channels of communication open with the Cuban government. Which obliquely implies the notion that relations with Cuba might have been different if JFK had not been murdered.

With the Johnson administration bogged down in an "unwinnable war" in Southeast Asia and Civil Rights battles occurring on the streets of the US, Cuba and its revolution began to fall off the radar. By 1964, the Johnson administration, concerned with public opinion, as mentioned, took swift and immediate action to stop the deliberate terror perpetrated on the Cuban people. LBJ, in April of that year, called for a cessation of sabotage attacks. Johnson openly admitted, "We had been operating a damned Murder, Inc., in the Caribbean.'"[121] Nonetheless, the national security apparatus (i.e., the CIA, the Joint Chiefs, and military intelligence) along with US policymakers (and US-based exile groups), remained obstinate, steadfast, and consistent in their goal – to punish (if not kill) Fidel Castro and his revolution, by maintaining a punitive program of economic strangulation with the hopes that Castro would be, not only

---

[119] "378. Memorandum From Gordon Chase of the National Security Council Staff to the President's Special Assistant for National Security Affairs (Bundy)," in *FRUS*, 1961–1963.

[120] Julian Borger, "Revealed: How Kennedy's Assassination Thwarted Hopes of Cuba Reconciliation," *Guardian*, November 26, 2003.

[121] Michael McClintock, *Instruments of Statecraft: U.S. Guerilla Warfare, Counter-Insurgency, Counter-Terrorism, 1940-1990* (New York, 1992), 205.

isolated on the world stage, but condemned by his own people who would rise up and eradicate the man and his socialist regime – which did not occur. Of course, the termination of hostilities directive ordered by Johnson did not include economic enmity - which persisted throughout the 1960s and beyond. In fact, a CIA field agent appointed to anti-Castro operations detailed the agency's sadistic objectives as expressed through author John Marks, by explaining:

"Agency officials reasoned, ... that it would be easier to overthrow Castro if Cubans could be made unhappy with their standard of living. 'We wanted to keep bread out of the stores so people were hungry ... We wanted to keep rationing in effect....'"[122]

The purpose of the economic blockade remained fixed from the early 60s onward: to contain, defame, discredit, and destroy Castro and his experimentation with, what the US considered, subversive Communist ideals.

Finally, the US's belligerent, if not insidious, hardline stance toward this small island nation reignited at the end of the 1960s, which included not only an economic strangle-hold, but full-blown underground sabotage operations. The 37th president of the United States, Richard M. "Nixon's first acts in office in 1969 was to direct the CIA to intensify its covert [Hybrid War] operations against Cuba."[123] Nixon and his then National Security Advisor, Henry Kissinger, still believed, callously, that military aggression, violence, brutality, and intimidation (coalesced by vicious economic sanctions) were the answers to America's woes abroad. US policy toward Cuba for more than sixty years is reminiscent

---

[122] John Marks, *The Search for the Manchurian Candidate: The CIA and Mind Control* (London, 1979), 198.

[123] Raymond Garthoff, *Detente and Confrontation: American-Soviet Relations from Nixon to Reagan* (Washington, DC, 1985), 76n.

of a famous quote often attributed to Albert Einstein: "Insanity is doing the same thing over and over again, but expecting a different result." Hence, Castro's Cuba (not only America's nemesis, but also the model of an uncompromising US global order) was the consequence of an even longer and persistent imperial US foreign policy: If the United States had not impeded Cuba's push for national sovereignty and self-determination in the initial part of the 20th century; if it had not sustained a sequence of tyrannical despots on the island; and, if it had not been complicit in the termination and manipulation of the 1952 election, an ineradicable character such as the young reformist, and socialist, Fidel Castro may never have materialized.[124] Ultimately, the headstrong US stratagem of assassination and suffocation of Castro and his socialist revolution failed, not only by bolstering his image on the island, but abroad as well. Ironically, the US helped to create its own oppositional exemplar of resistance, in the image of Fidel Castro, Che Guevara, and the Cuban people, i.e., the revolution - two men and a small island nation that stood up defiantly to the US led global-capitalist-order and would not relent. The US feared the Revolution of 1959's challenge to class power, colonialization; and, its popularity with the multitudes - thus, it had to be forcefully restricted through malicious policies of trade embargoes, threats of violence, and ideological isolation. In fact, the Cuban rebellion courageously and tenaciously stood up to, and resisted, specific contrivances (or designs) by which the US had customarily, boastfully, and self-admiringly delineated its dominant status through the forceful protection of its exploitative business practices (aka, the "Yankee boot") on the backs of the Cuban people, for which, Fidel Castro and his

---

[124] Stephen Kinzer, *Overthrow: America's Century of Regime Change from Hawaii to Iraq* (New York, 2007), 91.

bottom-up-populist-crusade were held ominously, insidiously and interminably responsible....

Chapter Five

BETTER DEAD THAN RED

By 1960, moderate conservatism, i.e., President Dwight D. Eisenhower's brand of temperate Republicanism had overshadowed the traditionalist views of Senators Robert Taft and Joseph McCarthy throughout the halls of power in Washington D.C., which led to a sense of alienation and marginalization by those members and their constituents that stood within the orthodox wing of the GOP, "As a result, that constituency began to organize at the grassroots. According to a conservative directory, for example, the number of right-wing groups more than doubled between 1957 and 1965—the largest number of which operated out of Southern California [slowly branching out nationwide]."[125] A single-candidate stratagem transpired within this "new conservative" movement of the early '60s and ultimately manifested itself in the form of one man: Arizona Senator Barry Goldwater – and his well-known brand of "cowboy conservatism." Goldwater was an ardent believer in the "American way of life" which, according to him and his followers, encompassed the principles laid out below in a way that not only exemplified the lone righteous path forward for the nation, but also stood as an exemplar of integrity, truth, and justice to the world. One of a long list of motivational factors sat at the heart of this

---

[125] Lisa McGirr, *Suburban Warriors: The Origins of the New American Right* (Princeton, 2015), 113.

movement's galvanizing behind a single candidate's vision of what defined "true conservatism" and their key to a winning strategy: electoral politics through grassroots mobilization - which they believed was the only path to affect national governance by bringing the nation back to the traditional values that had made it great: the spirit of entrepreneurialism; hard work; limited federal government; limited taxation; minimal regulations over business; the sanctity of private property; the inviolability of the individual; personal responsibility; states' rights; law-and-order; and, a strong and well-funded national defense. After the release of his book *The Conscience of a Conservative*, ghostwritten in 1960 by L. Brent Bozell brother-in-law of conservative *National Review* founder William F. Buckley, the book, and, the Senator both, became runaway hits – making Goldwater the nation's most prominent conservative. His doctrine of American fundamentalism strictly eschewed FDR's New Dealism; its progressive tax policy; the national welfare state; race and class issues; worker's rights; unions; and women's rights, as elements of socialism or worse yet "communism," which were a desecration detrimental to the unique freedoms enshrined, by the nation's framers, within the United States Constitution.

These sentiments were previously stressed in fellow arch-conservative Strom "Thurmond's Platform of the States' Rights Democratic Party, "[126] or Dixiecrats, a coalition of disaffected southerners within the Democratic Party that represented its ultra-conservative wing which shattered the Democrats' then Solid South in 1948, "We believe that the Constitution of the United States is the greatest charter of

---

[126] "Platform of the States' Rights Democratic Party," August 14, 1948, The American Presidency Project: https://www.presidency.ucsb.edu/documents/platform-the-states-rights-democratic-party.

human liberty ever conceived by the mind of man."[127] Thurmond, Governor of South Carolina from 1947 to 1951 and later US Senator, became the protuberant figure of states' rights and racial traditionalism, who in 1956 outlined a "Southern Manifesto" condemning school integration,[128] and later performed a record twenty-four-hour filibuster in contradiction to a 1957 Civil Rights bill.[129] What Thurmond made evident to the conservative right was that the race issue could place the South in play, meaning, "race" could help shift traditional white voters to the conservative cause, a factor that would become interlaced within conservative electoral politics for generations to come.

When it came to the race issue, Lewis Gould explains, ironically, that "Goldwater had supported the civil-rights laws of 1957 and 1960, but he stopped short on the 1964 proposal."[130] A staunch constitutionalist, the Senator "believed, based on the anti-civil rights views of such legal advisers as William Rehnquist and Robert Bork, that the measure was unconstitutional."[131] Goldwater took, what he alleged to be a principled stand and "decided that he would vote against the law in the Senate: 'The problem of discrimination cannot be cured by laws alone,' he told his colleagues. States' rights prevented the government from interfering with 'local issues' such as race relations."[132] In the

---

[127] Ibid.

[128] *The Declaration of Constitutional Principles*, Congressional Record, 84th Congress Second Session. (Washington DC, March 12, 1956).

[129] Nadine Cohodas, *Strom Thurmond and the Politics of Southern Change* (New York, c1993), 296–297.

[130] Lewis L. Gould, *The Republicans: A History of the Grand Old Party* (New York, 2014), 253.

[131] Ibid.

[132] Ibid.

end, Goldwater benefitted from white fear over the race issue in the South. As such, "every Republican presidential candidate after Barry Goldwater would reach out and seek to expand the new, white conservative base in the South that he had helped to create"[133] - what would later become known as the Southern Strategy. Which paradoxically took the shape of a sleight-of-hand in that, school integration was "wise and just" he declared, but federal courts imposing such a doctrine was a violation of "states' rights" which was intolerable from his point of view.[134] Ultimately, Goldwater's appeal to his white-southern conservative base took the form of fear-mongering, "The Civil Rights Act, he continued, would make the federal government into a 'police state' and would lead to 'the destruction of a free society.'"[135]

This Senator's extreme ideological fight for Americanism and his militant stance against the Soviet Union was succinctly summarized in his slogan "Better Dead Than Red," meaning, it was better for the nation to suffer a nuclear holocaust than to be ruled by communists. Thus, Goldwater believed, that the nation must strive to achieve and maintain military global dominance through the superiority of nuclear weapons.[136] In fact, Goldwater fumed against what he considered a lack of principle (in the form of capitulation) of so-called American liberalism, by stating, "The rallying cry of an appeasement organization, portrayed in a recent novel was, 'I would rather crawl on my knees to Moscow than die under an Atom bomb.'"[137] Thus, Anticommunism (or the belief in a

---

[133] David Farber, *The Rise and Fall of Modern American Conservatism: A Short History* (Princeton, 2010), 85.

[134] Barry M. Goldwater, *The Conscience of a Conservative* (Princeton, 2021), 17–24.

[135] Farber, *Rise and Fall*, 76.

[136] Goldwater, *Conscience of Conservative*, 107.

[137] Ibid., 86.

shared enemy), as Niels Bjerre-Poulsen affirms, became the "ideological glue" within the modern conservative crusade.[138]

Saber-rattling, bellicose posturing, and fear-mongering in American politics were in no way unique to Barry Goldwater. Previously, by 1950, after the Allied forces defeated Nazi Germany in World War II, the hopes and aspirations of most Americans seemed limitless. But with the acquisition of atomic weapons by the Soviets; Eastern Europe behind an "Iron Curtain"; and, Communist China victorious in anticolonial revolution, ominous signs lurked everywhere, including within the shadows of US national governance. In light of that, Senator Joseph McCarthy, in his 1950 "Lincoln Day Address," declared, "In my opinion the State Department … is thoroughly infested with Communists."[139] In this speech, McCarthy not only sowed the seeds of his own destruction but cultivated and promulgated a belief system that said communist sympathizers were there, behind the scenes, in all walks of American life – a belief system that undergirded, propelled, and persisted within America's "new conservatism," encouraging its rise to prominence. In addition, William Buckley, who David Farber asserts, "had more than any other individual strengthened the conservative cause,"[140] was the voice of the intellectual new-right and a McCarthy supporter, at least initially, who helped sustain that belief system, later avidly damning organized labor and "big government liberalism as a veiled variant of … communist evil."[141]

---

[138] Niels Bjerre-Poulsen, *Right Face: Organizing the American Conservative Movement 1945-65* (Copenhagen, 2002), 39.

[139] Joseph R. McCarthy, "Lincoln Day Address," February 20, 1950, available at:
http://www.historymuse.net/readings/lincolndayaddress.html.

[140] Farber, *Rise and Fall*, 75.

[141] Ibid.

Retrospectively, 1940 to 1947 saw union membership in the US surge from 7 to 15 million,[142] a trend that horrified conservatives by exemplifying a growing socialist presence in America. But a legislative land-mark victory, soon to come, would later help galvanize and inspire future generations of traditionalists to fight for their cause, i.e., the battle against "collectivism" in all its forms, hence summarized by Marc Dixon:

Business-led efforts to curtail unionism at the national level culminated in the highly restrictive Taft-Hartley Act of 1947. Among other things, the ... Act outlawed secondary boycotts, allowed for "employer free speech" during union election drives, [clamped down on communist infiltration], and ceded jurisdiction to the states in the regulation of union security and Right-to-Work laws.[143]

As Robert Mason verifies, "regulation of organized labor amounted to significant challenges to New Deal liberalism."[144] In fact, according to David Lawrence, founder of *U.S. News* (a long-time conventional publication), the Taft-Hartley Act was the first conservative victory in the long crusade to reverse, what conservatives believed to be, the dangerous socialist tide of the 20th-century New Deal. Lawrence proclaimed that, "America has turned away from state socialism, wherein the government is the master and the citizen is the servant,"[145] which was a succinct summary of a

---

[142] Leo Troy, "Trade Union Membership, 1897-1962," *The Review of Economics and Statistics* 47, no. 1 (1965): 93.

[143] Marc Dixon, "Limiting Labor: Business Political Mobilization and Union Setback in the States," *Journal of Policy History* 19, no. 3 (July 2007): 313.

[144] Robert Mason, *The Republican Party and American Politics from Hoover to Reagan* (Cambridge, 2011), 116.

[145] David Lawrence, "America Turns the Corner," *U.S. News*, July 11, 1947.

key factor of limited government woven within the philosophy of American conservatism past, present, and future. Moreover, as Bjerre-Poulsen queries, "So what, if anything, did Goldwater the ardent advocate of 'right to work' laws have to offer union members? Freedom from 'government interference.'"[146] In effect, by the early 1960s, and with the help of the "Senator from the West," small government rhetoric and right-to-work laws were directly absorbed and adopted in over twenty states across the US.[147] The new conservative movement was on the rise.

In the '60s, the conservative movement like the New Deal coalition, which remained in part throughout the 1950s, was an electoral coalition at its core, but it varied in variety and nature. Its electoral base was more racially alike but still diverse, merging business heads with southern suburbanites and northern manufacturing workers who were previously and consistently Democrats. Lisa McGirr exposes an interesting tactical alignment within conservatism made evident by the emergence, in the 1960s, of longtime Democrat and staunch segregationist, George C. Wallace. Wallace, an ardent anticommunist, also utilized, as McGirr explains, "the language of a lower-middle-class populism, [which] held deep attachments to New Deal programs, the welfare state, and unions—attachments that were anathema to most Southern California (as well as national) conservatives."[148] As a consequence of these partialities, conservatives, in Orange County and nationally, avoided third parties; and continued, to a great extent, committed to working with and within the Republican Party. However, Wallace's appeal to labor (or

---

[146] Bjerre-Poulsen, *Right Face*, 246.

[147] Dixon, "Limiting Labor," 319.

[148] McGirr, *Suburban Warriors*, 115.

working-class-populism) would later enshrine itself in conservative politics.

That said, from 1945 throughout the 1960s and beyond, Communism and/or "collectivism," stood as the central threat to obtaining what conservatives deemed a free and prosperous society where an individual (through entrepreneurism, "traditional values" and hard work) could reign supreme in his own life and reach his highest potential. As Bjerre-Poulsen confirms, "while anticommunism was only one aspect of conservatism, it was without a doubt the most important in terms of publicity and public support."[149] One organization that occupied this space and developed a lasting impact on the philosophy of individualism over the "disease of collectivism," embedded within the movement, by 1960, was Robert Welch's John Birch Society. The Birchers (as they were also known) became a principal grassroots conservative organization, with remarkable strength throughout the Southwest. Bircher hysteria (and/or extremism) branched out in all directions, stressing to its membership that "Communist infiltration and influence [continues] right inside our own continental borders ... unions which control our shipping, and many vital parts of our economy are Communist-ruled...."[150] This organization saw the fight for civil rights, and government support, as a method of "fomenting internal civil war" in the country, which was a form of aiding and abetting the Communist side in that war.[151] Another unifying factor within the movement's development was desegregation: The battle against "liberal judges," and specifically, the fight to impeach Justice Earl Warren (an Eisenhower appointee) who the Birchers saw as a supporter of integration which, in their

---

[149] Bjerre-Poulsen, *Right Face*, 57.

[150] Robert Welch, *The Blue Book of The John Birch Society* (San Francisco, 2015), 24.

[151] Ibid.

view, amounted to a Communist plot.[152] Ultimately, Welch took a step too far (in 1960) by circulating a text entitled, *The Politician* Welch, where he alleged that then President Eisenhower, himself, was "carrying out Communist orders,"[153] but this only partially discredited the society. For the most part, the organization remained formidable, motivating the members of the Republican party of Texas and California – which supported Goldwater in '64 and provided an active theme for Ronald Wilson Reagan (former actor turned political spokesperson) summarized in the group's slogan, "Less government and more responsibility."[154]

Reagan's televised speech *"A Time for Choosing"* (just prior to the election in '64) not only stood as an electrifying moment for the new conservative cause in general, but it aided Goldwater; and, furthermore, it shifted the center of gravity of the Republican Party from the old Northeastern Establishment to the newly established Sunbelt conservatives: "Goldwater's views, which in 1964 had been widely [regarded] as extreme … [would] become part of Republican orthodoxy. Most evident was his 'law and order' theme … after antiwar protests, inner-city-riots, and soaring-crime-rates, [had] revealed its true potential."[155] Reagan railed against excessive taxation, big government, welfare, and the Great Society – which later, in 1966, helped him become California's most popular Republican governor.[156] Reagan spoke the anti-communist language of the new conservative movement by pounding away at government bureaucrats, "There is only an

---

[152] McGirr, *Suburban Warriors*, 129.

[153] Robert Welch, *The Politician* (Belmont, Massachusetts, 1963), 109.

[154] Welch, *Blue Book*, 99.

[155] Bjerre-Poulsen, *Right Face*, 297.

[156] Totton Anderson and Eugene Lee, "The 1966 Election in California," *The Western Political Quarterly* 20, no. 2 (1967): 546.

up or down – up to man's old-age dream, the ultimate in individual freedom consistent with law and order – or down to the ant-heap [of] totalitarianism."[157] He demonstrated for his audience his political views with a "humorous anecdote" on the age-old antagonisms that lie between the haves and the have-nots and big government, "We have so many people who can't see a fat man standing beside a thin one without coming to the conclusion that the fat man got that way by taking advantage of the thin one. So, they are going to solve all the problems of human misery through government and government planning."[158] Reagan hit an emotional, if not motivational, nationalistic nerve within the grassroots conservative right by declaring, "If we lose freedom here, there is no place to escape to. This is the last stand on Earth."[159]

As Mason points out, grassroots organizing was nothing new to the Republican Party, in fact, it goes back to Senator Robert Taft's early 1950s bitter-uphill-battle against Eisenhower, "Arguments about the party's minority problem informed the battle between Eisenhower and Taft. Taft insisted that enthusing grassroots Republicans led to good organization, which in turn maximized the party's vote. The way to enthuse activists was via a stress on conservatism."[160] Goldwater, and his devotees, certainly those with a sound political memory, would, by 1960, take those consequential sentiments to heart. In fact, Mason continues, "It was not the power of his strategic argument that won the nomination for

---

[157] Ronald Reagan, "A Time for Choosing," October 27, 1964, Ronald Reagan Presidential Library: https://www.reaganlibrary.gov/reagans/ronald-reagan/time-choosing-speech-october-27-1964.

[158] Ibid.

[159] Ibid.

[160] Mason, *Republican Party*, 144.

Goldwater. Instead, it was the success of the pro-Goldwater movement within the party."[161] That said, although Goldwater lost big to President Lyndon Baines Johnson in '64, a committed grassroots conservative movement aimed at national power had taken shape.[162]

That committed character was personified by Phyllis Schlafly (an Illinois lawyer and ardent Republican activist), through the release of her seminal, pro-Goldwater, 1964 book, *A Choice Not an Echo;* and her staunchly anticommunist and antifeminist conservative newsletter, *The Phyllis Schlafly Report* – where, in the early 1970s, she espoused the imperative to stop the Equal Rights Amendment (ERA), which demanded equal-legal-rights for *all peoples* irrespective of sex in the workplace; educational opportunities etc. But Schlafly saw it differently, as she later outlined in a *Washington Star* interview:

> I think it is destructive.... I think their goals can be summed up ... as a takeaway of the legal rights that wives now have.... [It] is pro-abortion.... [and it] is pro-lesbian, which is certainly an anti-marriage movement ... So, I consider ... their principal objectives ... antifamily.[163]

Due to what she believed was the nation's descension into "moral depravity," Schlafly teamed up with Richard Viguerie, a fellow Catholic, who pioneered, in the early 1960s, an innovative fund-raising-technique through a mass mailing stratagem that penetrated into an array of largely conservative Christian organizations and societies later

---

[161] Ibid., 191.

[162] Farber, *Rise and Fall*, 85.

[163] Judy Flander, "Interview with Phyllis Schlafly," *Washington Star*, January 18, 1976.

known as the "Moral Majority."[164]According to Robert Freedman, this movement spawned, "from a combination of factors: the reduction of sectarian tensions that enabled different denominations to engage in common pursuit of moral reform via the political process ... and a reaction against the growth of social liberalism in the 1970s."[165] As a result of their efforts and reach, the ERA amendment fell short of the 38-state requirement for approval - which represented a huge victory for not only Schlafly and Viguerie, but also for the New American Conservative movement as a whole.

Industry is a factor that also needs to be highlighted here given its effects on demographic shifts, "new growth industries in defense and electronics not only to Orange County but also to other regions in the West and South,"[166] were a major boon to the conservative right in sheer numbers alone, since "the older northern industrial cities of the East and Midwest saw a decline in their manufacturing base. The resulting demographic ... changes would eventually help shift the balance of economic and political power in the nation increasingly southward and westward."[167] In fact, the new conservative campaign spread throughout the territory, in a grassroots style, focusing primarily, at least initially, in the sphere of the middle class, "...the rank-and-file cadres [of southwestern] communities - the housewives, doctors, engineers, dentists, and businessmen who had come into public view some years earlier to fight the collectivist menace in their schools [and] churches..."[168] – now, trudged the streets of their districts successfully disseminating literature

---

[164] Farber, *Rise and Fall*, 130.

[165] Robert Freedman, "Uneasy Alliance," in *Seeking a New Majority*, ed. Mason and Morgan (Nashville, 2013), 125.

[166] McGirr, *Suburban Warriors*, 27.

[167] Ibid.

[168] Ibid., 112.

and ideas on conservatism and its disposition. Farber unveils an interesting motivational factor woven within the movement's commitment. On the one hand, by '64, "...Goldwater had been a flawed candidate. His ill-considered talk of atomic bombs and Asian land wars had given the liberals [i.e., President Johnson] the language with which to mock him, transforming his campaign slogan from 'In your heart, you know he's right' to 'In your guts, you know he's nuts.'"[169] But on the other hand, Goldwater had undeniably inspired a generation of conservative activists by teaching them the grit and political power of "bare-knuckles [cowboy] conservatism."[170]

The battle of influence and ideas (in the war of Right vs. Left ideology) would certainly span decades, climaxing in a late 1960s left-oriented "counterculture" that included an antibusiness, antiwar, antipoverty, and pro-environmental stance which rattled corporate America and business leaders across the country. After the GOP's slim Presidential victory in 1968, Richard Milhous Nixon, who Adolph Reed Jr. argues, did more for the American left than any subsequent Democratic President (in the form of Environmental Protection, Affirmative Action and Occupational Safety and Health standards etc.),[171] would deal a severe rightward blow to that war of ideas (in the form of a long-term win for the new conservative movement), by appointing renowned corporate lawyer Lewis F. Powell Jr. to the Supreme Court. Earlier, Powell had laid out, in his 1971 "Confidential Memorandum" (the Powell Memo), a corporate-oriented; well-funded, systematic approach to capitalism's triumph over "socialism"

---

[169] Farber, *Rise and Fall*, 85.

[170] Ibid.

[171] Adolph Reed, "Why Labor's Soldiering for the Democrats Is a Losing Battle," *New Labor Forum* 19, no. 3 (October 1, 2010): 14.

- not by winning politically, but by influencing the public mind: "Strength lies in organization, in careful long-range planning and implementation ... [central to that planning was] the role of the National Chamber of Commerce"[172] and other corporate organizations, think-tanks etc. - in countering what Powell considered a broad attack on the "free-enterprise system." That methodical organizational effort included: staffing right-wing scholars at universities; reevaluating textbooks especially in the Social Sciences; and "the FBI's yearly publication [and evaluation] of speeches made on college campuses by avowed Communists."[173] But it did not stop there. According to Powell, the national television networks and other outlets including radio, scholarly journals, national publications, and paid advertisements should be "monitored" in the same way that textbooks should be kept under strict surveillance – to systematically submerge the rhetoric of the "New-Left."[174]

Finally, the seeds of future successes of New Conservatism had been firmly sown in the fertile soil of the 1960s with a social-issues (antiestablishment) movement on "the left," again, demanding an end to the Vietnam War; environmental safeguards; civil rights for African Americans and women's rights etc. - manifesting in the form of domestic unrest (in urban areas and on college campuses) which propelled the Right to organize against, in their view, the collectivist ramifications, cultural polarization and racialized leveling of LBJ's "Great Society." In addition, as Mason states, "This [counter] Social Issue [movement] also involved

---

[172] Lewis F. Powell Jr., "Memorandum: Attack On American Free Enterprise System," August 23, 1971, available at: https://law2.wlu.edu/deptimages/Powell%20Archives/PowellMem orandumTypescript.pdf.

[173] Ibid.

[174] Ibid.

issues of ... 'permissiveness,' subjects like drug use and sexual behavior,"[175] from which the new conservative crusade, by the end of the decade, became galvanized, organized and mobilized (with the support of business leaders and politicians alike) in terms of strategy, ideas, networks, and communications: "[A] movement, which first mobilized middle-class men and women to action against the communist menace, had reconstructed itself [on moral grounds] earning a new political respectability."[176] This repackaging of the conservative movement's image across the American political landscape later shifted its language from "us and them" to "We the People," which propelled the social conservative cause to new heights not seen since the late New Deal era. With this newly found influence in hand, the movement began immediately to implement all steps, it believed, would help tear down what remained of the "communist-inspired" New Deal mandate. That said, political scientist, Everett Ladd intimates, "[this] tendency toward increasing conservatism within the [Republican party's] ideological journey ... left it decreasingly well equipped to communicate with ordinary voters who were generally more centrist."[177] Nevertheless, armed with a powerful belief in the free market system, meshed within a strident religiosity or moral rectitude, this New-Right struggle would find itself not on the fringes of the American mainstream, but assimilated as a mainstay in American culture - culminating in a "clean-sweep" in 1981 in the form (of the small-government doctrine) of one man: Ronald Wilson Reagan, summarized as "the Reagan Revolution," a fierce reaction against the "malaise" of the late

---

[175] Mason, *Republican Party*, 218.

[176] McGirr, *Suburban Warriors*, 260.

[177] Quoted in Mason, *Republican Party*, 245.

1970s.[178] Reagan,, embodying the spirit of Goldwater and all the aspirations of the new conservative movement, optimistically placed the country on a steadfast and broad conservative trajectory, social, economic and military, for which the movement was ecstatic. In fact, George Will (conservative political commentator), famously summarized the Goldwater/Reagan nexus, per the former California governor's Presidential win, by stating, "we ... who voted for him [Goldwater] in 1964 believe he won, it just took 16 years to count the votes...."[179]

---

[178] Farber, *Rise and Fall*, 128.

[179] George Will, "The Cheerful Malcontent," *Washington Post*, May 31, 1998.

Chapter Six

WHAT HOLLYWOOD COMMUNICATES THROUGH THE MOVIE GREEN BOOK: Race, Ethnicity, National Identity, Gender, Culture and Class in 1962 America

As a core tenet of supranationalism, Daniel T. Rodgers proclaims, "A nation which conceives of itself in exceptionalist terms is fated to spend at least as much of its popular historical energy imagining everyone else's history as in writing its own."[180] This aphorism is essential when it comes to understanding David R. Jansson's application of Edward Said's theory of "Orientalism." According to Said, "the Orient has helped to define Europe (or the West) as its contrasting image, idea, personality, experience."[181] Jansson explains that, for this dynamic to work, the West must be uniquely positioned as separate and distinct from that of the Orient. This apposition among geographical areas is what undergirds "difference": a delineation of the "other" external to the state[182] which stirs as Said argues, "elaborate theories,

---

[180] Daniel T. Rodgers, "Exceptionalism," in *Imagined Histories: American Historians Interpret the Past*, ed. Anthony Molho and Gordon S. Wood (Princeton, N.J: Princeton University Press, 1998), 24.

[181] Edward W. Said, *Orientalism* (New York: Vintage Books, 1979), 1–2.

[182] David R. Jansson, "Internal Orientalism in America: W.J. Cash's *The Mind of the South* and the Spatial Construction of

epics, novels, social descriptions, and political accounts concerning the Orient, its people, customs, mind, destiny, and so on."[183] Jansson expresses "internal orientalism" as the opposite poles of a binary: a spatial, regional or geographical area internal to a state which is defined by its distinct cultural identification that lies outside the hegemonic norms or values associated with the state itself.[184] As James C. Cobb emphasizes, "Typically, the creation of any sort of group identity, be it regional, national, ethnic, or otherwise, has required ... a 'negative reference point,' against which it may be defined in stark and favorable contrast."[185] Jansson focuses largely on W.J. Cash's influential work, *The Mind of the South* (1941) , from which he argues, "Portrayals of the South such as Cash's denote [it] as the repository of a set of negative features (such as poverty, racism, violence and backwardness), and that ... these undesirable characteristics are excised from the national identity."[186]

Jansson describes Cash's innate and interminable "southern" features, "Violence, intolerance ... attachment to racial values and a tendency to justify cruelty and injustice in the name of those values...,"[187] as not only southern features, but national characteristics which exist throughout the United States as a whole. He declares that by disregarding the long

---

American National Identity," *Political Geography* 22, no. 3 (March 1, 2003): 295.

[183] Said, *Orientalism*, 2–3.

[184] Jansson, "Internal Orientalism in America," 293.

[185] James C. Cobb, "Introduction," in *Away down South: A History of Southern Identity* (Oxford University Press USA, 2005), 3.

[186] Jansson, "Internal Orientalism in America," 293.

[187] David R. Jansson, "'A Geography of Racism': Internal Orientalism and the Construction of American National Identity in the Film *Mississippi Burning*," *National Identities* 7, no. 3 (September 1, 2005): 270.

and tortured history of cultural and geographical neglect through the advantage of a hegemonic yet illusory sense of preeminence the U.S. in no way ameliorates the historical conditions that create an internal orientalism but only exacerbates them. Jansson argues, "This [mythic] national identity [of purity, righteousness, modernity and justice for all is misleadingly] reproduced through the daily activities of the academy, media, political system, entertainment industry and other institutions."[188]

Similarly, Joseph Crespino focuses on the state of Mississippi as the misconceived epitome of "southern-ness" in the mind of the nation. He defines Mississippi "exceptionalism" as a racialized extreme, a uniquely insular, violent and authoritarian society within a society that was separate and distinct from the U.S. in the 1960s. He describes Mississippi's most noxious image as a metaphor of a "closed society"[189] conversely assessing the nation itself as a metaphor of "Mississippi-Writ-Large": The state of Mississippi and its long history of ugly racism, bigotry, violence, discrimination and segregation is intrinsic to its regional character in an abhorrent way, but when compared to that of the nation's long history of brutal racial intolerance as a whole, it in no way stands alone.[190]

This essay evaluates the frameworks of internal Orientalism, the closed society and Mississippi-Writ-Large as depicted in Hollywood's award-winning film *Green Book* (Peter Farrelly, 2018) and its representations of a geography of racism; southern vs. national identity; place and space; and

---

[188] Ibid.

[189] Joseph Crespino, "Mississippi as Metaphor: Civil Rights, the South, and the Nation in the Historical Imagination," in *The Myth of Southern Exceptionalism*, ed. Matthew D. Lassiter (Oxford: University Press, 2010), 100.

[190] Ibid., 105.

the us vs. them distinction. These frameworks similarly contain and maintain the edifice of a mythic national identity as a consequence of the "othering" of the American South. This work also examines, through a 21st-century Hollywood lens, race, ethnicity, gender, culture and class in 1962; the societal representations and anthropological interplay, which mold contemporary popular perceptions, woven within this film's illustrations and interpretations.

Green Book starring Mahershala Ali (as Dr. Donald Shirley) and Viggo Mortensen (as Tony "Lip" Vallelonga) was written by Nick Vallelonga (et al.), the son of the real-life "Lip" who long desired to tell the story of his father's and Don's unique experience.[191] Inspired by true events, the film starts out in 1962 Bronx, New York, focused on the character of Tony "Lip" Vallelonga, a white-working-class husband and father of two who is employed as a bouncer at the renowned nightclub the Copacabana. Tony's character is that of an ethnically clichéd northeastern Italian-American: a hard-working family man, uneducated and unsophisticated; prejudicial if not racist; uncouth and ill-mannered; violent when need be; good with his fists and not afraid to use them. Tony's nickname "Lip" is a moniker that he wears proudly – it was given to him by his childhood friends due to his distinct rhetorical abilities to "bullshit" or persuade anybody anywhere of anything. Due to these innate gifts Tony is sought out, interviewed and hired by Dr. Don Shirley an a-typical African American character as far as 20th century perceptions go: Don is refined, well-educated; well-read; cultured and urbane; a globally recognized extremely skilled musician. Green Book is something of a dark comedy, a cultural and phenotypical odd couple hit the road together in a 1962 semi-

---

[191] Andrew R. Chow, "What to Know About the Controversy Surrounding Green Book," Time, February 24, 2019, https://time.com/5527806/green-book-movie-controversy/.

segregated and racially charged nation at large. Only one year prior, in 1961, Black and white protestors, known as Freedom-Riders, rode buses throughout the American South demonstrating against segregated "whites-only" public toilets, lunch counters and bus terminals – their struggles were met by gruesome and overt violence from white separatists.[192]

Thus, Don is in need of not only a chauffeur but a strongarmed troubleshooter who is willing and able to escort him on a two-month concert tour for elite-white audiences through middle America, down across the segregated South and ultimately straight into the heart of the Mississippi Delta. The actual *"Green Book"* on which the film is titled was named *The Negro Motorist Green Book* (1936-1967) and was the brainchild of Victor Hugo Green an African American postal worker in New York City who saw the need for a "safe-haven" publication: a list of hotels and motels throughout the continental U.S., in the Jim Crow era, that were disposed to providing accommodations to African American travelers.[193] The book is central to the film's storyline in that it provides Don's chauffeur Tony a specified list of locations, per their journey, where Doncan spend the night without fear of being arrested for violating racial codes or social mores within a particular jurisdiction – this racialized paradigm is fundamentally thematic throughout the film.

The movie opens with a sequence of scenes that help the viewer to solidify the character of Tony "Lip." He is seen at the Copacabana urgently summoned to a brawl over "a broad"

---

[192] Thomas F. Jackson, *From Civil Rights to Human Rights: Martin Luther King, Jr., and the Struggle for Economic Justice* (University of Pennsylvania Press, 2007), 141.

[193] Michael Ra-Shon Hall, "The Negro Traveller's Guide to a Jim Crow South: Negotiating Racialized Landscapes during a Dark Period in United States Cultural History, 1936-1967," *Postcolonial studies* 17, no. 3 (2014): 307–319.

where Tony forcefully pulls a man out of the club, throws him in the street and knocks him unconscious. Next, we see Tony returning home to his humble abode only to find numerous family members vigilantly watching over is petit wife Dolores (tenderly played by Linda Cardellini) who is shown to be genteel enough to provide two African American workmen cool glasses of water on a hot summer day which Tony promptly and wincingly tosses in the trash upon their departure - clearly demonstrating a subtle yet albeit northern racist character.[194]

The first encounter between the two protagonists is a telling one. Don receives Tony at his posh apartment perched above Carnegie Hall in Manhattan. This scene is set up to jar the viewer by drawing a sharp contrast, contrary, to mid-20th century societal norms per not only race but class. Don sits suspended upon a throne dictating the required duties necessary to fulfill the position, i.e., driver, personal attendant, valet and baggage handler. Tony, feeling offset or crestfallen by this dynamic from the very start, indignantly responds:

> ...I ain't no butler ... I'm not shining nobody's shoes. You need someone to get you from point A to point B? You need someone to make sure there's no problems ... and you going through the deep South ... there's gonna be problems...[195]

---

[194] Jeanne Theoharis and Komozi Woodard, "Introduction," in *The Strange Careers of the Jim Crow North: Segregation and Struggle Outside of the South*, ed. Brian Purnell (New York: University Press, 2019), 2.

[195] Nick Vallelonga, Brian Hayes Currie, and Peter Farrelly, *Green Book (Screenplay)* (Dreamworks Pictures, 2018), 18, accessed March 7, 2021, https://www.scriptslug.com/assets/uploads/scripts/green-book-2018.pdf (all further dialogue is from this screenplay).

This dialogue helps to highlight nationally embedded themes of not only an exceptionalist South set apart from national norms but a "geography of racism" that is unique or innate to the southern character as purported by Cash, "violent, racist, intolerant ... cruel, unjust ... and close-minded,"[196] which undergirds the "us and them" distinction that contrasts the nation with the South, as argued by Jansson, strengthening archetypal American virtues.

Don, desperate for a driver that can fulfill his needs, cajoles Tony by calling his wife Dolores directly asking permission to take her husband away for two long months and she consents. In delineating gender roles, the writers shrewdly include this 1950s/60s working-class trope emphasizing the wife "as the boss."[197] With the two men on the road headed toward Indiana we get our first hint of "othering" northern style – demonstrating in racial terms how Black culture was viewed as monolithic. Tony, bewildered by Don's lack of knowledge concerning Black pop music, flips through radio stations querying him, **"How could you not know this music?** Chubby Checker, Lil' Richard, Sam Cooke, Aretha - - these are your people!"** Don sports a nervous smile giving viewers their first oblique indication of a self-conscious sense of distance from "his own people" due to nothing other than class, as A.O. Scott, *The New York Times* film critic observes, "[his] hauteur masks a deep loneliness,"[198] which will become more evident as the film unfolds. Next, Tony finds himself

---

[196] Jansson, "Internal Orientalism in America," 307.

[197] Lynn C. Spangler, *Television Women from Lucy to Friends: Fifty Years of Sitcoms and Feminism* (Westport, Conn.: Praeger, 2003), 54.

[198] A. O. Scott, "'Green Book' Review: A Road Trip Through a Land of Racial Clichés," *The New York Times*, November 15, 2018, https://www.nytimes.com/2018/11/15/movies/green-book-review.html.

arguing with a stage manager at a university campus in Indiana as to whether the piano they have is up to snuff – Tony demands a Steinway (which is written into Don's contract), the stage manager glances smugly and says, "Come on, what's the difference -- **these coons can play on anything.**" Tony slaps the man hard across his face promptly ending the debate. He quickly becomes, as Scott points out, "a kind of 'white-savior,' intervening to shield his employer, when he can, from white people who have no such obligation."[199] This scene demonstrates Jansson's counterview to the prevailing mythic national identity, illuminating overt racial prejudice in the North.

The film employs a series of segments depicting cultural stereotypes and class distinctions. Although Don is perturbed, Tony is elated to purchase Kentucky Fried Chicken "in Kentucky" for the first time in his life, "I bought the bucket so you could have some." Don crossly responds, **"I've never had fried chicken in my life."** The writers lay out, with a 21st-century irony, a litany of clichés concerning bigoted white attitudes in the 1960s toward African American culture generally and their food and musical tastes in particular. As Adolph Reed states, "[throughout American history] … race essences generally were thought to include – in addition to distinctive physiognomy – values, attitudes, and behavior."[200] When Tony pulls over beside a cotton field in North Carolina, for an engine check, one is taken aback not only by the riveted Black "pickers" working the field in amazement to see a Whiteman chauffeuring a Blackman in 1962 America, but also Don's own discomfort with his status or position given their reaction – his sense of estrangement is confirmed.

---

[199] Ibid.

[200] Adolph L. Reed, "The Underclass Myth," in *Class Notes: Posing as Politics and Other Thoughts on the American Scene* (New York, NY: The New Press, 2000), 96.

Arriving at their first show in the South (an elegant plantation home) for an audience of elite-white southerners, Don is not only dejected by the southern fried chicken prepared in his "honor," but he is also shown an outhouse if he should need a restroom facility. Seven years after Rosa Parks sat down to stand up against injustice on a Montgomery Alabama bus in 1955,[201] African Americans were still unable to share restroom facilities throughout the South. Don, guided by the *Green Book,* is forced to stay at run-down Blacks' only motels finding himself face-to-face with poor African Americans – the class distinction is palpable.

Subsequently, Tony is urgently called by Don's bandmate to a local "shit-hole-dive-bar" where a group of southern "rednecks" have Don physically pinned to the bar after having roughed him up, bloodied his face and threatened him with a knife. Tony appears, with a gun behind his back, demanding they let him go while the rednecks, portrayed as unhindered, violent, and degenerate, wildly mock the two of them:

> **REDNECK #1:** This **boy's** gonna get what's coming to him … you ain't got no say!
>
> **LIP:** Maybe. But, whatever happens, I'm gonna put **a bullet** right in … **that thick skull of yours.**

This encounter exemplifies what Cobb describes, "was the white South captured so brilliantly by W. J. Cash [as] … a savagely racist, intellectually stunted, emotionally deranged society…"[202] Tony's white-savior characteristics peak in this scene. The rednecks back down and the two men walk out of the bar as Don quips, **"Does geography really matter? … If I walked into a bar in your neighborhood…, would it be**

---

[201] Jackson, *From Civil Rights to Human Rights,* 53.

[202] Cobb, "Introduction," 1.

any different?" Farrelly smartly sustains a stark contrast visually in place and space while, at the same time, using this sequence to tacitly acknowledge violent racism in the North as referenced in Crespino's Mississippi-Writ-Large metaphor.

Thus far, and in the scenes that follow, "The South is [largely] represented as a landscape of violence ... intolerance and hatred, corruption and complicity ... [contrary to the] mythical American national identity."[203] Now, decisively in the deep South, the "southern mentality" of racism is offered as a common occurrence through the eyes and experiences of the film's protagonists. Walking through Macon Georgia, Tony sees an attractive suite in a shop window that he thinks would be perfect for Don. The shopkeeper swiftly explains that Don Don, being Black, is not permitted to try anything on without paying for it first - the two men, disgruntled, swiftly exit the shop.

Don's pensive awkwardness manifest throughout the film is made tangible, given the fervently oppressive cultural mores of early 1960s America – which 21st-century observers may find revelatory at best and/or tyrannical at worst. Tony appears in a Macon, GA YMCA restroom where Don is being humiliatingly detained by local police for engaging in a consensual liaison with another man. The writers demonstrate, unequivocally, for the first time, that Don is not only a Blackman, but a "gay" Blackman coexisting in a highly racialized and repressive epoch. Thus, Don's inclinations throughout the storyline, e.g., helping Tony write tender and meaningful love letters to his wife; his artistic view of the world in general, and his sensitivity toward beauty in particular, so conveyed, are essential to his nature – which, although cliché, will make sense to contemporary audiences. Back at the hotel, after having bribed the two police officers

---

[203] Jansson, "Internal Orientalism in America," 307.

into letting Don go, Tony warmly (and unexpectedly) projects an empathy and/or benevolence toward Don, hitherto not seen in the film, by submissively stating, **"I know it's a complicated world out there...."**

Driving along a desolate Mississippi road at night in the pouring rain the duo is pulled over by two white patrol officers that explain to Tony, **"He [Don] can't be out here at night. This is a sundown town."** Meaning that Black folk are not allowed outside after dark. The patrol officer asks Tony the origin of his last name and he responds "Italian," the officer retorts, "Oh, now I get it. **That's why you driving this boy around... you half a nigger yourself."** Tony spontaneously punches the officer landing himself and his boss in a Mississippi jail. Don is reluctantly permitted his one phone call, as per the law, and immediately reaches out to Attorney General Robert Kennedy in Washington, DC, who contacts the governor who in turn contacts the sheriff - the two men are promptly released. This scene exemplifies the binary of internal orientalism as defined by Jansson. By juxtaposing the South, the image of Robert Kennedy represents an intervention on behalf of justice and the American way - a righteous national image and superior national character that contrasts and supersedes any and all relationship with the lesser of the two.[204]

As tensions build between the duo, Don's class and racial identity crises alluded to earlier in the film are exhibited for all to see. Class distinctions are made clear as Tony claims to be more in touch with "Black culture" than Don given his elevated status, "You travel around the world and live on top of a castle and do concerts for rich people! I live on the streets ... **my world is way more blacker than yours,"** with this statement, the writers interpose, through a racialized lens, the

---

[204] Ibid., 300.

20th-century stereotype of a "racially afflicted underclass," i.e., whites equating Black culture, nationwide, with poverty more than anything else.[205] Monique Judge, African American film critic for *The Root*, labeled Tony's declaration as "clueless and offensive,"[206] however, after having had the first bi-racial African American president, Barack Obama, in what is purported as a "post-racial era," the writers skillfully word Don's poignant response in a way that 21st-century audiences (Black and white) can not only understand, but relate to:

> Yes, **I live in a castle! Alone.** And rich white folks let me play piano for them, because it makes them feel cultured. But when I walk off that stage **I go right back to being another nigger to them** … that is **their true culture. And I suffer that slight alone** … I'm not accepted by my own people … I'm not like them either! **So if I'm not black enough, and I'm not white enough, and I'm not man enough, what am I?!**

If viewers were wondering why Don drinks himself to sleep every night, this scene clarifies his deep emotional wounds per "detachment and disconnectedness" from not only his race but his class. In the subsequent and final scenes, the writers focus primarily on race and space emphasizing regional differences to underscore the "mind of the South" through a North/South distinction. Don finds himself at the final show of the tour, a Birmingham hotel, where he is to perform that evening, again, for an elite-white southern audience. The maître d'hôtel attempts to rationalize to Don the fact that, although he is a distinguished guest, he, unlike Tony and his bandmates, is not allowed to eat among the other

---

[205] Reed, "The Underclass Myth," 96.

[206] Monique Judge, "*Green Book* Has Great Acting, a Misleading Title and Palatable Racism for White People," *The Root*, November 20, 2018, https://thegrapevine.theroot.com/green-book-has-great-acting-a-misleading-title-and-pa-1830572839.

guests in the dining area – it goes against the hotel's "long-standing tradition." The maître d' clarifies southern culture and racial attitudes, "**...this is just the way things are done down here.**" As in Crespino's closed-society metaphor, this representation exemplifies the South as a land apart "different" and "out of step with the rest of the country."[207] The two quickly find themselves on the road headed back to the "civilized" North.

As Jansson states, "The US is composed of many regions, which have been defined in various ways ... and for one of these regions [i.e., the South] to serve as an internal "other" it must be distinguished from national standards."[208] Consequently, in a heavy snowstorm the two men are, again, pulled over by a patrol car (intended to heighten the viewer's fear of southern authority), but this time it happens to be a white Maryland State Trooper who kindly assists Tony while he changes a flat tire stating (to both Tony and his African American boss), "**Okay... be careful, gentleman. Merry Christmas.**" Contrary to the maître d' and the white southern cops, the northern State Trooper represents "the archetypal American ... tolerant ... enlightened and modern,"[209] accentuating "national identity." Lastly, we see Don outside Tony's apartment door where he is greeted by a bearhug from Tony and a kiss on the cheek from his wife Dolores – who lovingly thanks him for helping her (semiliterate) husband write his weekly letters to her. Although his large-Italian-American family is seated, around the holiday dinner-table, stunned at the fact that a tall Blackman is standing in their foyer, Johnny (a relative of Tony's) exclaims, "**Well, come on, make some room, get the man a plate.**" Everyone laughs

---

[207] Crespino, "Mississippi as Metaphor," 102.

[208] Jansson, "Internal Orientalism in America," 299.

[209] Ibid., 311.

and welcomes him in – the writers climax with an "all-is-well" 21st-century "post-racial" Hollywood finale, again, reinforcing a mythic national identity.

Ultimately, *Green Book* is much more than an "on-the-road" dark comedy. The movie permits 21st-century audiences to view race, ethnicity, culture, gender, and class - plus regional and national identity - through the eyes of its protagonists in 1962. Depicted only one year after Martin Luther King Jr. moved from Montgomery to Atlanta to devote more time to the SCLC and the freedom struggle,[210] Farrelly could have communicated a story which included the hard-fought battles, trials, and tribulations, of African Americans throughout the civil rights period in which the film is set but instead decided to leave those issues and events principally aside. In fact, Judge laments, "The instances of racism in this film [are] mild compared to the actual racial terrorism black people experienced then and continue to experience."[211] Nonetheless, viewers will walk away satisfied that the film's central theme, a stark contrast between the North and the South was evidently delineated; and, that the American national mythology was definitively manifest and pronounced. Per Judge's point, this essay in no way means to diminish or trivialize the long southern legacy of white terror, promulgated and protected by the political, social and legal structures, rained down upon African Americans throughout the region, as V.O. Key empirically states, racial bias and power concentration was manifest in the South at the highest echelons of authority, "The critical element in the structure of black-belt power has been the southern Senator and his ... right to veto proposals of national intervention to protect

---

[210] Jackson, *From Civil Rights to Human Rights*, 105.

[211] Judge, "*Green Book* Has Great Acting."

Negro rights."[212] Jansson does not deny this viewpoint, but expounds upon it, "if the collection of vices considered, as a whole, to be uniquely Southern can be contained within the South, then they can be washed clean from the national identity."[213] Crespino points out, "The failure of the closed society metaphor was not ... its description of Mississippi, but [its] refracted image of America." Thus, in respect to this film, the frameworks presented in this essay force one to re-consider the big picture highlighting the southern character vs. the national myth dichotomy (which makes evident a collective amnesia) per the factual role of "America" in the 1960s due to deliberate distortions per actual crimes that have transpired and continue to transpire outside the South.[214]

---

[212] V. O. Key and Alexander Heard, *Southern Politics in State and Nation*, New ed. (Knoxville: University of Tennessee Press, 1984), 9.

[213] Jansson, "'A Geography of Racism,'" 268.

[214] Jansson, "'A Geography of Racism,'" 280.

Chapter Seven

IDEOLOGY AND HYPOCRISY AMID SLAVERY AND DEMOCRACY
Strange Bedfellows from Time Immemorial

The history of the existence of slavery as an institution in antiquity and beyond is one of the most common; and, at the same time, one of the most complex tales to be told. Virtually every society, touching almost all the continents of the world, has had its own form of enslavement. The implication being that, nearly, every group of humankind whether racially, ethnically, or culturally categorized as diverse, unattached, or essentially separate, has been marked by the legacy and tradition of human bondage geographically and/or ancestrally. This work will be focusing on the origins and culturally supportive underpinnings of ancient Greek identity, its philosophy, law, ideology, and ethnicity; and, those extant essentialist elements, such as class, that not only made slavery in the ancient Greek world possible but normalized its place within a societal hierarchy that helped define who and what an ancient Athenian was - pitched against a broader Mediterranean ethos. Beyond that, this work will address how ancient Greek thought, as to what essentially constituted a slave versus a free person, later ignites a heated counterpoint which asserts hypocrisy lies at the core of ancient Greek thinking when it comes to the fundamental differences: physical, psychological, and emotional, that inexorably lie between free-persons and human-beings in captivity – made evident by how that debate rages to this day in contemporary historiography....

It is best that we start at the beginning with Homer: ancient Greek storyteller and legendary poet, who lived as early as the 8th century BCE; and, is still considered one of the most celebrated and influential writers of antiquity - for good reason. Homer is brought to the fore because his illustration as evidenced below reveals the essential deleterious effect of human bondage, which, poignantly foreshadows the debate mentioned above by millennia, 'For Zeus who views the wide world takes away half the manhood of a man, that day he goes into captivity and slavery' (Homer, *Odyssey* 17.367-9). Homer is explicitly defining the enslavement of a man as the diminishment, in a purely ontological sense, of one's inherent human dignity. Aristotle, on the other hand (ancient aristocratic Greek philosopher and polymath extraordinaire), who penned his work in the latter 4th century BCE, some four hundred years after Homer, sets a foundational opposition and enduring precedent of his very own when it comes to the quality, status, value, and condition of enslaved persons.

Aristotle, as is broadly known, defined an enslaved person (*doulos*), that is, a human being held in bondage, as 'a live article of property' (Aristotle, *Pol.* 1253b33). The great thinker himself, speaking on behalf of his class interests, goes on to define the value he derived from such persons *defined as property*, 'Of property, the first and most indispensable kind is that which is ... most amenable to Housecraft; and this is the human chattel.' He then goes on, with a decisively imperialist tone, 'Our first step therefore must be to procure good slaves (*doulous*)' (Arist. *Oec.* 1344a23-26). Aristotle makes clear his essentialist views which not only defined a slave as property, but goes further, stating that the value, status, utility, and material condition of persons classified as slaves is not only a useful one, but *a natural* one:

These considerations therefore make clear the nature of the slave and his essential quality; one who is a human being (*anthrôpos*) belonging by nature not to himself but to another is by nature a slave, and a human being belongs to another if, although a human being, he is a piece of property (*ktêma*) (Arist. *Pol.* 1254a14-18).

Aristotle's proposition is an important one given this work's purpose which is to bring forth these precise notions, or conflicting theories, that have significantly undergirded, influenced and/or reinforced conceptions of class, personhood, value, and status interwoven within Western thought throughout the ages.

Which brings us inevitably to the longstanding property versus domination argument spearheaded, in modern scholarship, by Orlando Patterson in his 1982 book entitled *Slavery and Social Death*. Patterson delivers a scathing rebuke to Aristotle's customary formulation of slavery in terms of property. He unequivocally argues that slavery, from his learned vantage point, is, in fact, 'the permanent, violent domination of natally alienated and generally dishonored persons'[215]. Which poignantly parallels Homer's description that human beings, held in captivity against their will, are not only persons dominated physically, but are individuals essentially diminished morally, emotionally, and psychologically. The conventional view, as presented by Aristotle, is unsound, according to Patterson based on two distinct factors. Firstly, Patterson argues, 'to define slavery … as property fails as a definition, since it does not really specify any distinct category of persons.' Because everyone, whether 'beggar or king, can be the object of a property relation.' One

---

[215] Orlando Patterson, *Slavery and Social Death: A Comparative Study* (Harvard University Press, 1982), 13.

can only construe that what Patterson is saying, when it comes specifically to slavery, is that the term 'property' obscures, diminishes or diverts one's attention away from the overt and brutal nature of an enslaved person's everyday lived experience. Secondly, Patterson contends that the term property is inconsistent in substance when it comes to diversity of culture - meaning many societies, however archaic, lacked the very concept of ownership. Denoting that slavery has accompanied mankind through time immemorial, from primitive village societies to ancient Mesopotamia and beyond, where, he argues, the laws and social mores of any given society didn't precisely match that of Aristotle's definition of property – therefore it generally fails as a classification of slavery.[216]

David M. Lewis counters Patterson's argument on the 'property point' as stated above by proclaiming that during the Neo-Babylonian and Persian periods, the evidence clearly demonstrates in abundant detail, that the circumstance between slave and master, in legal terms, was 'a relationship based on the fact that the slave was the property of his or her owner'-exhibiting all the elementary features necessary, per legal theory, to reach the standard of 'property.'[217] Lewis challenges Patterson's stance further by stating:

> [The popular] view that esteems private property rights to be an advanced development of Roman legal theory ignores the findings of almost a century of legal anthropology, which has observed private property systems in a variety of tribal social systems that were far less advanced in terms of

---

[216] Patterson, 20–21.

[217] David M. Lewis, *Greek Slave Systems in Their Eastern Mediterranean Context, c.800-146 BC*, First edition. (Oxford, United Kingdom: Oxford University Press, 2018), 34.

technological and social complexity than even the society imagined in Homer's epics.[218]

While Lewis' examination proves 'slavery as a form of property' in a legal context, there is still validity in Patterson's position given the fact that persons in bondage (from a humanist perspective) reduced to the level of property in a solely 'legal sense' nullifies their individual agency and all that essentially makes them human.

In fact, slavery, and democracy, in ancient Athens and beyond is a multidimensional and multifaceted story of innate human capacity and agency, dignity, adaptability, fortitude, and resistance. Meaning, '…slaves were not passive objects, whose identity and existence were completely dominated by their masters.'[219] As described by Xenophon (Greek military leader and philosopher), there were without a doubt slaves forced into strenuous domestic work: 'baking, cooking, spinning' and scrubbing under their owner's will (Xen. *Oec.* 9.9). That said, we are also told of others that gained valuable skill-sets outside the home, coinciding with their inherent intelligence and creativity, from potters to builders to bankers and shoemakers (Hyperides, 3.1-9; and Aeschines, 1.97)[220]. These slaves participated in communal undertakings (such as workshops and spiritual associations) together with other free and enslaved persons. Even Aristotle, who had little love (*agape*) for the underclasses, had to acknowledge, albeit cautiously, the inherent *democratic nature* (and/or threat thereof) made evident by the sheer numbers of this uniquely collective phenomenon - what the great theorist himself

---

[218] Lewis, 39.

[219] Kostas Vlassopoulos, "Greek Slavery: From Domination to Property and Back Again," *The Journal of Hellenic Studies* 131 (2011): 195.

[220] Edward E. Cohen, *Athenian Economy and Society: A Banking Perspective* (Princeton University Press, 1992), 61–109.

branded as *koinônia,* simply defined as fellowship of the masses. But the *politikê koinônia* (he warns) was specifically formed for the *benefit* of its members (Arist. *Eth. Nic.* 1160a4-6). Influenced by his celebrated teacher, renowned philosopher Plato, who argued that the limits of citizenship and its influence correlate with 'the precise form of constitution and law' in place (Plato, *Laws* 714c) - Aristotle's well-known anti-democratic discourse on *'mob-rule'* and the necessity for the 'rule of law' as fundamental to 'the natural order of things' thus becomes most evident. While in agreement with Pericles' famed proclamation on the importance of the 'rule of law' in the ancient Greek city-state; when it came to what Pericles professed as the virtues of democracy defined, the two-men parted ways in dramatic fashion. In what is considered the ideal of a democratic philosophical vision, Pericles outlines *demokratia* (in his famed funeral speech of 431 BCE), as follows:

> Its administration favors the many instead of the few...equal justice to all...class considerations not being allowed to interfere with merit; nor again does poverty bar the way. The freedom which we enjoy in our government...[teaches] us to obey the magistrates and the laws, particularly as regard [to] the protection of the injured (Thucydides, 2.37).

On the contrary, Aristotle's depiction of a 'democratic regime' and/or constitution is one with an inherent propensity toward 'license and lawlessness.' He defines, 'radical democracy,' in that of Athens for example, as having two critical flaws: firstly, the influence of the *demos* can potentially supersede the law (Arist. *Pol.* 1292a4ff.); and secondly, the *demos* hold the power to impeach magistrates for wrongdoing (such as malfeasance) which Aristotle intimates are both a step too far (Arist. *Pol.* 1292a30, and cf.1298a29-35). That said, as threatening as he might have interpreted it, the concept of *koinônia* permits us to observe enslaved persons actively utilizing their intrinsic agency within a broader collective milieu.

Returning to the question as stated at the outset of this work, Lewis' focus on the laws of ancient societies, in lieu of the contention outlined above, is immensely valuable when it comes to understanding the conventions per Athenian slave society and their ramifications. Broadly viewed as a protection mechanism for slaves, given a singular example, the Greek law on 'hybris,' in ancient Athens, expressly defined as the negation of the *deliberate* implementation of violence to humiliate, demean, or degrade - is not as straightforward as it might appear. Yet again, hypocrisy abounds as evidenced: to presume that the Athenian law pertained to an owner's misconduct toward his 'property' obliges us to disregard the 'abundant proof' of regular and generally habitual violence toward slaves by their masters (Lewis, 2018, 43). Beyond that, it is difficult to correlate the law as 'protectionary' given this evocative assertion by Plato, '[a slave] when wronged or insulted, is unable to protect himself or anyone else for whom he cares' (Plato, *Gorg.* 483b). The following statement is as definitive as it gets when revealing the underlying deceit interwoven within Athenian law itself when it came to enslaved persons and their standing, '[the] law included slaves [simply] because the lawgiver wished to curtail the spread of hubristic [or anti-social] behaviour among the citizens *tout court* … the hubris law was designed to engender respect and orderly conduct among citizens *not* to protect slaves.' [221] [222] Meaning, that the Athenian lawgivers were not overly concerned with the physical well-being of persons classified as slaves, but perhaps were more intent on curtailing their judicial workload.

The reality was that the right of masters to physically abuse their slaves in ancient Athens was, if not absolute, certainly extensive. Xenophon affirms the practical necessity on behalf of owners to punish their slaves, but simply asks for them not to do so in a state of rage (Xen. *Hell.* 5.3.7; cf. Hdt. 1.137). Demonstrating that, violence toward persons in bondage in ancient Athens was perfectly acceptable if it was executed in a manner of equanimity. According to Xenophon, however, slaves should never resist. He goes on to say, that masters could, or should, 'clap fetters on them so that they can't run away' (Xen. *Mem.* 2.1.16). Hence, so it is argued, in summary, that what helps clarify, or defend, Aristotle's assertion that 'the slave [is] an article of property imbued with a soul' (Arist. *Pol.* 1253b32), *is justified* due to the fact that 'this view of the slave as an article of property' was a generally held belief of society at large when it came to the status of enslaved persons within the ancient Greek ethos.[223]

That said, when it comes to hypocrisy, the law and excessive abuse–domination, as defined by Patterson permeates the historical record. A poignant example of the common acceptance in ancient Athens of emotional and physical abuse (or the threat thereof) cast upon slaves, and the like, is provided by Lysias, where he describes in detail the

---

[221] Mirko Canevaro, "The Public Charge for Hubris Against Slaves: The Honour of the Victim and the Honour of the Hubristēs," *The Journal of Hellenic Studies* 138 (2018): 100–126.

[222] Lewis, *Greek Slave Systems in Their Eastern Mediterranean Context, c.800-146 BC*, 42–43.

[223] Lewis, 54.

testimony of a plaintiff in an Athenian court recounting the brutal (and pervasive) threat of torture (and even death) that hung over the heads of enslaved mill workers - commonly known 'as mill-roaches' (Lysias 1. 18-22). In addition, owners of enslaved persons were generally granted legal leeway, under the authority of judges, to sexually abuse their slaves.[224] Signifying that when a slave was purchased, they were in fact the owners' possession to do with as they desired - which helps lend even more credence to Patterson's analyses of domination as described.

A question of further importance is what defined, or signified, a slave and their station in ancient Athens? Was it one of ideology or innate difference that helped delineate the distinction between a Greek and a non-Greek? As understood in the broadest sense of the term, *barbarian* is the word used to describe not only a non-Greek speaking immigrant, but in fact, a definitional term which explicitly portrayed an enslaved person of foreign origin, as, 'non-Greeks imported from foreign lands via the slave trade'[225]. An Athenian essentialist view, as noted, between native slave and foreign slave, (that is, between natural-born Greeks and outsiders) is underscored by Aristotle's description of an enslaved Greek as 'an accident contrary to nature' (Arist. *Pol.* 1255a1). These Greek essentialist views, of one people's ethnic superiority over another, are noteworthy because they significantly impact Western thought and societal conditions throughout the ages – emphasizing race and class as inherent points of difference develop into a clear normative of class hierarchy.

Fast forwarding to the 18th-century Anglo world for example, Francis Hutcheson (elite 18th-century British moral

---

[224] Lewis, 42.

[225] David M. Lewis and Mirko Canevaro, "Poverty, Race, and Ethnicity," in *A Cultural History of Poverty in Antiquity (500 BCE – 800 AD)*, ed. Claire Taylor (Bloomsbury).

philosopher) proclaimed that permanent enslavement *should be* 'the ordinary punishment of … idle vagrants.' 'Idle vagrants,' being defined as most anyone with what Hutcheson considered, 'slave like attributes,' from the idle poor and indigent to confiscated and subjugated human cargo - principally Africans.[226] Conversely, in something of a confessional, Thomas Jefferson (slave owner, philosopher, and 18th century American statesman) recognized and voiced the odious elements of the dominion argument, as defined, some two hundred years prior to Orlando Patterson, '[the] commerce between master and slave is a perpetual exercise of … the most unremitting despotism on the one part, and degrading submissions on the other.' He then goes on in a revelatory tone, to inform just how these elite classes, throughout the millennia, bequeathed attitudes of dominion from one generation to the next. Stating that, the children of the elite were thus 'nursed, educated and exercised in the daily art of tyranny.' Virginia's slave plantations as he describes, were by their very nature, 'schools of iniquity and domination'[227]. Consequently, Aristotle's, early, and pervasive, theory of the 'natural order of things,' when it comes to class and ethnicity, is made brazenly evident (Arist. *Pol.* 1252a-1253b).

Finally, how commonplace was slave society in the ancient Greek world and what was its magnitude? It is said that the importation of slaves was a lasting one, being that Greek slave society lasted enduringly throughout both the archaic and classical periods until its absorption by Rome in 146 BCE. Although the Roman slave trade surpassed that of

---

[226] Edmund S. Morgan, *American Slavery, American Freedom: The Ordeal of Colonial Virginia* (New York: Norton, 1995), 324.

[227] Thomas Jefferson, *Notes on the State of Virginia: An Annotated Edition, Notes on the State of Virginia* (Yale University Press, 2022), 249.

the Greek numerically, given Rome's imperial might over the Mediterranean world, it is said that 'the Greek slave system was both the elder and the longer-lived.' The Greeks had helped set a historic precedent by perfecting their own imperial prowess through the conquering of their neighbors.[228] But, where in fact were these subjugated and enslaved persons extracted from and how common were they in ancient Greece? Ancient Greek inscriptions help make evident that enslaved peoples, represented a wide breadth of humanity throughout the known world at the time. These people included men, women, and children in a variety of hues, from such far-off places as Thrace, Phrygia, Syria, Caria in southwest Anatolia, Illyria on the western Balkan Isthmus, Scythians from eastern Iran; and, Colchians from the eastern Black Sea [229] - depicted by Herodotus, in the 5th century BCE, as a 'dark-skinned and woolly haired' people (Hdt. 2.104.2). What Herodotus' quote helps to highlight for us is an ancient Athenian social construct. That being, the prevalent belief (when it came to the stature of imported slaves), of a clear and innate delineation based on race (and/or phenotype), accentuating a natural taxonomic classification or difference between indigenous Greeks and all others – especially slaves.

When it comes to how common slaves were, Josiah Ober estimates the slave population of fourth-century BCE Athens to be around 35 percent of the total population of roughly 227,000. [230] Which made slavery quite pervasive throughout ancient Athens and helps to explain the essentialist Greek/Other dichotomy as such. As Vincent Rosivach makes

---

[228] Lewis and Canevaro, "Poverty, Race, and Ethnicity," 7.

[229] Lewis and Canevaro, 4.

[230] Josiah Ober, "Inequality in Late-Classical Democratic Athens: Evidence and Models," in *Democracy and an Open-Economy World Order*, ed. George C. Bitros and Nicholas C. Kyriazis (Cham: Springer International Publishing, 2017), 129–129.

evident, '[When] Athenians thought about slaves, they
habitually thought about *barbaroi*, and when they thought
about *barbaroi* they habitually thought about slaves'[231].
Suggesting that this was commonplace in classical Athens -
legislatively undergirded by the proposed law of Pericles of
451 BCE which confined citizenship solely to persons of
Athenian birthparents on both sides. Ultimately defining in
ethnocentric terms, an essentialist difference (between Greeks
and others), based on birth lineage and cultural origin (Arist.
Const. Ath. 26.3). In paralleling slave societies throughout the
epochs, 'the slave system of the fourth-century Greek world
was of roughly the same numerical magnitude as that of the
United States ca. 1800.' By the early 19th century, in the
South, '30-40 percent of the population' was made up of
chattel slavery under the brutal control of concentrated wealth
and political power, land, and resources.... [232] Both societies
(separated by millennia) became indulgently rich and
hegemonically powerful in their respective spheres of
influence – primarily based on the wealth created by their
slave societies thus implemented. As mentioned, due to the
commonality of the everyday interaction between slave and
non-slave, and its oblique dangers in ancient Athens, elite
class interests reinforced 'the construction of local and wider
Hellenic ethnicities, as well as of non-Greek ethnicities, must
have been fundamentally imbricated with the ideological
needs of the slave trade....'[233] [234] The main point being that

---

[231] Vincent J. Rosivach, "Enslaving 'Barbaroi' and the Athenian
Ideology of Slavery," *Historia: Zeitschrift Für Alte Geschichte* 48,
no. 2 (1999): 129.

[232] Peter Kolchin, *American Slavery, 1619-1877* (New York:
Hill and Wang, 1993), 242.

[233] Lewis and Canevaro, "Poverty, Race, and Ethnicity," 15.

[234] Thomas Harrison, "Classical Greek Ethnography and the
Slave Trade," *Classical Antiquity* 38, no. 1 (2019): 36–57.

the possibility of a unifying or coming together of freeborn citizens, of lower-class status, and slaves, posed a direct structural (and numerical) threat to the established order of things. Ideology, woven within Greek identity, plays a key role in the hegemonic control of social norms, but not an absolute one.

The understanding by the masses (and a small number of elites alike) that extreme concentrations of wealth played a destabilizing role in the Athenian political and social realms, when it came to privilege, power, and class, is made obvious by the following quote from Demosthenes, 'for the *demos* to have nothing and for those who oppose the *demos* to have a superabundance of wealth is an amazing and terrifying (*thaumaston kai phoberon*) state of affairs' (Ober, 1990, 214; Dem. *Ex.* 2.3). Which helps make evident an ancient Athens as not only the well-known paradigm of direct democracy (or rule by the many), but also its intrinsic contradictions (or threats thereof) when it came to status, class, and wealth – which has echoed, as argued, throughout the centuries. As presented, Lewis and Canevaro, bring to the fore, a carefully crafted top-down societal prejudice designed to sow division amongst the masses using class distinctions and/or differences as its exclusionary tool of choice:

> Since it was in fact slaves who were more naturally associated with manual labor—they were the prototypical manual laborers— elitist writers and reformers found in this proximity a productive avenue for attacking their suitability for political participation—for having a voice. For elite Greeks and Romans this was a productive strategy for

denigrating and dehumanizing 'the poor' in political as well as daily life.[235]

Paradoxically, these notions of disdain toward the poor (or the slavish), defined (mostly) by the ancient Greek elite as, 'anyone who had to work for living' (Arist. *Pol.* 1277b5-7; 1255b23-38), were not limited to the Athenian upper classes. In fact, as Lucia Cecchet suggests, due to the sheer force of elite ideological thought and its pervasive influence (in the 4th and 5th centuries), even within the jury courts of democratic Athens, the repulsion of poverty (including slaves) became commonly offered as a widely conventional view, 'a *communis opinio* that the rich and poor shared alike' [236]; attitudes that permeate Western societies to this day, making evident, the powerful effects of elite capture through hegemonic cultural influence in ancient Athens and beyond.

In conclusion, throughout Western history, ancient Athens has been viewed as the ultimate model of democracy in a political, ideological, philosophical, and ethical sense – as presented in this work. At the same time, hypocrisy, pertaining to these epitomes of democracy (*demokratia* – or rule by the *many* – as outlined by Pericles), adversely permeated its upper classes and beyond with lasting ramifications. Thucydides, Plato, Aristotle and Xenophon, for example, were all critical of democracy, focusing their ire upon the populous; the possibility of its bad decision-making; and (what they believed to be), as 'the [intrinsic] ignorance ... of the *demos*, demagoguery and civil strife' [237]. Again, these

---

[235] Lewis and Canevaro, "Poverty, Race, and Ethnicity," 29–30.

[236] Lucia Cecchet, "Poverty as Argument in Athenian Forensic Speeches," 2013, 61.

[237] Ober quoted in Mirko Canevaro, "Democratic Deliberation in the Athenian Assembly: Procedures and Behaviours towards Legitimacy," *Annals HSS 73*, 2019, 3.

great theorists thought of democracy not as the rule of the many (which was the general Athenian ideal of *demokratia*), but they portrayed it in a more threatening or hostile sense, such as, 'the rule of the poor or the mob,' which helps taint Athenian *demokratia* within recorded history with a prejudicial top-down class perspective throughout the millennia. [238] The proximity between, slave and poor within the democratic confines of ancient Athens, made them susceptible, in both high-level institutional deliberation and, sometimes, in daily collaborations, to manipulative stratagems which 'aimed to denigrate and even disenfranchise them by stressing the "slavish" nature of their occupations, as incompatible with the virtue required for political participation.' [239] Furthermore, enslavement, as implemented in ancient Athens and across time, populations and locations could differ enormously or, in fact, possess significant similarities. As is inferred, by ancient Greek scholars throughout this work, the characteristics which helped mold Greek slave culture and its expansion comprised, but were in no way limited to, the amount of prosperity slavery added to the fundamental aspects of that society's supposed wellbeing, especially its economic growth and military strength. In most instances, throughout the ancient world and beyond, the capturing and subjugation of persons classified as slaves were meant to possess, chastise, and/or diminish an economic rival. Thus, as noted, chattel slavery was quite widespread throughout the ancient world and beyond. That said, the agency and humanity, as offered by Orlando Patterson, of subjugated persons, and their relentless struggle for freedom

---

[238] Mogens Herman Hansen, *The Tradition of Ancient Greek Democracy and Its Importance for Modern Democracy*, Historisk-Filosofiske Meddelelser 93 (Copenhagen: Det Kongelige Danske Videnskabernes Selskab, 2005), 8.

[239] Lewis and Canevaro, "Poverty, Race, and Ethnicity," 29–30.

permeates the historical record (from Athens to Virginia) - which cannot and should not be ignored. Enslaved human beings left behind a powerful legacy of opposition and struggle to free themselves and the family members they so loved. Through the common bond (of unrelenting misery) they forged powerful alliances of resistance and revolt, despite the cultural forces arrayed against them – their historical age or geographical setting.

Chapter Eight
GOVERNANCE, RACE, PROPERTY AND PROFIT

"Slavery is associated ... with the emergence of several of the most profoundly cherished ideals and beliefs in the Western tradition." ~ Orlando Patterson

The subjugation and forced enslavement of Black bodies seized from the continent of Africa had been fundamental to the expansion and growth of the Atlantic domain since the early fifteen-hundreds. In fact, African enslavement had been a mainstay throughout the Spanish Atlantic world for more than a generation prior to English colonization in the Americas. Seeing the Spanish not only as rivals for land, wealth, and resources, the English (not having yet invented their own legalized system of slavery) could also view them as a model concurrent with their French equivalents.[240] Thus, by the seventeenth century, the English had to create and/or erect the administrative and legal arrangements necessary to manage and control, what was for them, a new labor institution of power and governance. This essay will engage with and examine the intricacies and nuances which undergirded the legalized and culturalized formulations of

---

[240] Edward B. Rugemer, "The Development of Mastery and Race in the Comprehensive Slave Codes of the Greater Caribbean during the Seventeenth Century," *The William and Mary Quarterly* 70, no. 3 (2013): 432.

dominance, suppression, and supremacy, over African slave labor through the mechanisms of social control woven within European thought: race, law, class, religion, and revolt – immorally and hypocritically counterbalanced by both arbitrary freedoms for the few, and strict coercion for the multitudes, alluded to by the Orlando Patterson quote above.

Barbados, as esteemed Yale history professor Edward Rugemer asserts, was the codified starting point for racialized slavery in the Atlantic world. The development of racializing enslavement originated hither, but it remained incomplete. As early as 1636, the Barbados Council "excluded Europeans from the group who could be bound for life," but, as Rugemer specifies, "...they did not yet assume that all Africans or Indians who arrived would be slaves."[241] However, the ancient Aristotelian concept of "the natural slave"[242] was certainly well-known by British upper classes of the day as being anyone compelled into "forced labor for life" vs. the then novel British formulation of "contracted indentured servitude." In July 1636, Barbados' Governor Henry Hawley and his Council initiated perpetual slavery by proclaiming that "Negroes and Indians, that came here to be sold, should serve for life..."[243] Hence, Black Africans and indigenous peoples were formally and authoritatively deemed "natural slaves." Consequently, at this initial juncture in the island's socioeconomic development, and thenceforth, "Barbadians [clearly] made distinctions between those who served for life and those who worked under a contract."[244] Sir Hilary Beckles

---

[241] Rugemer, 433.

[242] Aristotle, *Politics*, trans. Harris Rackham, Loeb Classical Library (Harvard University Press, 1944), 1254b20.

[243] William Arnold, *Memoirs of the First Settlement of the Island of Barbados, and Other the Carribbee Islands ...* (near Chancery-Lane, Holborn: E. Owen, 1743), 20.

[244] Rugemer, "The Development of Mastery," 433.

(well-known Barbadian historian) underscores the fact that "sugar production" combined with the legally sanctioned concept of "unfree labor," were, in reality, the two sinister and compelling forces behind Barbadian planters' avarice and wealth accumulation.[245] In fact, the succeeding generations of Englishmen in Barbados favored themselves with certain freedoms per property and ownership which would embrace a racialized African enslavement; and, a system of coercive order and violence that suited their rapacious needs.[246]

As demonstrated below, history never runs in a straight line. If we take a closer look at reputable historical texts such as (seventeenth-century English author) Richard Ligon's *A True & Exact History of the Island of Barbados* (first published in 1657), we find innate elements that capture the imagination and move against a traditional narrative. From Ligon's on-the-ground perspective, having lived in the island of Barbados (from 1647 to 1650), he believed that temporary European contracted servitude was treated worse than Negro slaves who happened to be in subjugation for life. Ligon held that "servants were treated worse than the slaves." As a matter of fact, he delineated their poor nourishment and insufficient lodging (in detail); and, outlined the viciousness of their overseers who would, as he stated, "beat a Servant with a cane about the head 'til the blood ran freely."[247] In contrast to Ligon's assessment, one cannot help but be stunned by the wanton intimidation and legalized measures of violence enacted within "An Act for the Better Ordering and

---

[245] Hilary McD. Beckles and Andrew Downes, "The Economics of Transition to the Black Labor System in Barbados, 1630-1680," *The Journal of Interdisciplinary History* 18, no. 2 (1987): 225–47.

[246] Rugemer, "The Development of Mastery," 433–34.

[247] Richard Ligon, *A True and Exact History of the Island of Barbados*, ed. Karen Ordahl Kupperman (Indianapolis: Hackett, 2011), 94.

Governing of Negroes" (Barbados 1661), included in the larger work of *Acts Passed in the Island of Barbados* (from 1643 to 1762), which was published in 1764 and edited by Richard Hall Esq., Representative in the General Assembly for the Parish of St. Michael's Barbados. These texts reveal the gruesome and dreadful particulars of the then African slave's everyday lived experience.

The Acts mentioned provide the horrid and graphic details which challenge Ligon's assertion stated above. Race and religion are key elements woven throughout the law which not only defined Africans as "heathenish and brutish," but clearly delineated all white Europeans (owners and servants alike) as "Christians," which endowed them with certain divinely endorsed legal privileges - unmistakably demarcating skin-color as the dividing line of natural God-given rights, freedoms, and protections.[248] For example, in Clause II of the Barbados Act of 1661, the elite white "men of letters" that authored the proclamation openly delineated the punishments, and threats, thereof, legally sanctioned upon Negro men (and women alike) if they were to enact "violence to any Christian [including white servants] by striking or the like." Said slave shall be "severely whipped," his or her "nose shall be slit" and finally he or she shall be "burned in the face." Beyond that, they described Africans as "an uncertain dangerous pride of people ... to whom we may extend the legislative power [of punishment given us by Law] for the benefit and good of this plantation."[249] As they concluded, "property rights" and "ownership privileges" imbued within English law, originating from the Magna Carta of 1215,

---

[248] Stanley L. Engerman, Robert L. Paquette, and Seymour Drescher, eds., "An Act for the Better Ordering and Governing of Negroes" Barbados 1661, in *Slavery* (Oxford University Press, 2001), 105-106.

[249] Engerman, Paquette, and Drescher, 105.

authorized an Elite justification of such malicious violence toward Africans specifically. And, as Rugemer points out, "Slavery was essential, profitable to those invested in it, and fundamentally at war with the humanity of the people enslaved."[250]

War is by no means an exaggeration. If we look at the progression of legal mechanisms enumerated in Richard Hall's work, we find an evolution of ownership, coercion, and control largely instituted by, not only the ravenous want of financial reward on behalf of the English governing class of the island, but an innate fear of Africans as a people and the possibility or threat of their insurrection. For further illustration, Hall affirmed that the first official law implemented proclaiming Africans as not only chattel, but non-persons considered objects of ownership - took place as early as 1668, in "An Act declaring the Negro-slaves of this Island, to be Real Estates," to be displaced, utilized, traded, and controlled under a strict system of rule.[251] This stringent system of control and the governing class fear it stimulated, led to an even more severe lock-down in "An Act for the encouragement of all Negroes and Slaves that shall discover any Conspiracy," passed in 1692. Used as an overt force of intimidation, this Act was implemented to discourage, supplant, or suppress any notion of insurrection on behalf of

---

[250] Edward B. Rugemer, *Slave Law and the Politics of Resistance in the Early Atlantic World* (Cambridge, Mass: Harvard University Press, 2018), 2.

[251] Richard Hall, ed., "An Act Declaring the Negro-Slave of This Island, to Be Real Estates" Barbados 1668, in *Acts, Passed in the Island of Barbados. From 1643, to 1762* (London: printed for Richard Hall, 1764), 64–65.

all Africans; and, to stamp-out any and all risks of "Rebellion, Massacre, Assassination and Destruction."[252]

Those that write the rules control the game. Even prior to 1691, the white ruling class eminently dreaded the possibility of rebellion by African slaves thus harshly treated and controlled throughout the island. In fact, by 1661, they had already doubled down on their intimidation tactics, woven within legislative dictates, by instituting Martial law (that being, the replacement of civilian government by military rule). As revealed in Clause 17 of the Barbados Act of 1661, which distinctly stated, "if any Negro shall make Insurrection or rise in rebellion ... proceed by Martial Law against the Actors ... and punish [them] by death or other pain as their Crimes shall deserve."[253] Furthermore, the legislators specified within the law not only the punishments to be meted out, for the above-stated crime of insurrection, but also the benefits to be had. Specifically, a sanctioning by law which they had introduced per the loss of their property (said slaves) to be incurred by the public as a whole, "*It is* further enacted and ordained that the loss of Negroes so executed shall be born by the public."[254] They (the owner class) provided themselves with remuneratory safeguards and protections (outlined in Clause 18) - an indemnification backed by a self-serving tax strategy, which fell heavily upon the lower class tenants of the island, "when the present Treasury is not sufficient to satisfy the loss (of said property), a public Levy [is] to be presently made upon the Inhabitants for reparation

---

[252] Richard Hall, ed., "An Act for the Encouragement of All Negroes and Slaves That Shall Discover Any Conspiracy" Barbados 1692, in *Acts, Passed in the Island of Barbados. From 1643, to 1762* (London: printed for Richard Hall, 1764), 129.

[253] Engerman, Paquette, and Drescher, "Barbados Act of 1661" 110–11.

[254] Engerman, Paquette, and Drescher, 111.

of the same." ,[255] Which clearly demonstrated the power, influence, freedoms, and duties possessed by a minority of English elite propelled by a structure of primitive accumulation.

Coercion and law as divisive weapons of war. In response to the lingering possibility of a slave revolt on the island of Barbados, in 1676 the Assembly added draconian amendments to the 1661 "Act for the Better ordering and Governing of Negroes." In said amendments racialized difference and abhorrent essentialist qualities were openly demarcated as a tool of division and control which clearly placed the Negro slave at the bottom of the so-called "civilized social order" - even in the eyes of poor indentured whites. The Assembly's reasoning was justified within the preamble to the 1676 amendments which noted that the 1661 act "hath not sufficiently proved to restrain them [African slaves] from those wicked and barbarous actions their natures are inclined to ... [such as] thefts and insolencies."[256] Hence, as Susan Dwyer Amussen confirms, any form of larceny or assault committed by a slave was proclaimed a capital offense as outlined in the original Act. Beyond that, any enslaved individual "who remained a fugitive for more than a year" stood to be summarily executed when apprehended.[257] In a tactical move by the governing class, the coercive purpose behind the law was to increase the threat of punishments for slaves' wrongdoings in the hope that deterring minor offenses

---

[255] Engerman, Paquette, and Drescher, 111.

[256] Quoted in, Susan Dwyer Amussen, "Right English Government: Law and Liberty, Service and Slavery," in *Caribbean Exchanges : Slavery and the Transformation of English Society, 1640-1700* (Chapel Hill: The University of North Carolina Press, 2007), 135.

[257] Susan Dwyer Amussen, 136.

would thwart greater ones such as mutiny or revolt.[258] Island authorities and Planters relied on a similar blend of terror and coercion to force the increasing slave population into brutal compliance. Again, as alluded to by the Orlando Patterson quote at the outset of this essay, western values authorized violence within the law which necessitated the brutal relationship between masters and slaves.

Sugar, when it came to the possession and enslavement of Black bodies, was a complex and fundamental ingredient within the development of a system of perpetual slavery essential to the economic progress of the island of Barbados and beyond. A small number of planters commenced experimenting with sugar as early as the 1640s and, at the same time, London brokers who were already ensconced in transatlantic trade founded a commercial slave venture (The Royal African Company) to the island of Barbados straight from Africa. The numbers below prove that English capital accumulation stood at the heart of the ruthless capture and enslavement of Black Africans, "By 1643 there were 6,400 Africans on the island, about one-fourth of a population of at least 25,000, and by 1650 the European population had grown to about 30,000 while the number of Africans had increased to 12,800."[259] Estimates reveal that sugar, by the 1660s, had elevated the population of the island of Barbados to a majority black slave society – which is reflective, as discussed above, within a series of punitive Acts adjudicated on the island throughout the seventeenth century and the palpable numerical fears Africans instilled.

---

[258] Amussen, 135.
[259] Rugemer, "The Development of Mastery," 434.

Figure I[260] Figure II[261]

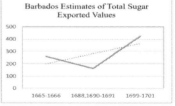

Barbados Disembarkation Estimates of African Slaves (1665-1701)

Years*	Disembarked Slaves
1665-1666	7108
1688,1690-1691	6354
1699-1701	16169

Estimated Values of Total Sugar Products Exported from Barbados (1665-1701) (in Thousands of Current Pounds)

Years	Sugar Tot. Values
1665-1666	259.6
1688,1690-1691	163
1699-1701	423.5

Barbados Estimates of Disembarked Slaves

Barbados Estimates of Total Sugar Exported Values

*Slave-Trading Voyages Barbados, 1665-1701. Data are one-year running averages that are combined to parallel the Sugar Exported Values in Figure II.

The data above, extracted from The Trans-Atlantic Slave Trade Database, corroborate a direct association between the increased importation of forced African slave labor and the export of the island's most profitable crop, as made evident by David Eltis' "New Estimates of Exports from Barbados…, 1665-1701." The figures show a 154% increase of disembarked Africans from 1688 to 1701, which directly corresponds to a 166% upsurge in the estimated values of total sugar products exported from Barbados in the same period.

From early on, the menace of punishment, coercion, and revolt were always present on the island of Barbados, but as Jennifer Morgan outlines, with the development of sugar manufacture and the increase in the African population -

---

[260] "The Trans-Atlantic Slave Trade Database (Voyages Data Set)," "Estimates" spreadsheet, 2023, http://www.slavevoyages.org/estimates/pUjAsKJW.

[261] David Eltis, "New Estimates of Exports from Barbados and Jamaica, 1665-1701," *The William and Mary Quarterly* 52, no. 4 (1995): 631–48.

things got worse.[262] Stemming from Oliver Cromwell's re-conquest of Ireland in 1641, thousands of Irish were sent to Barbados as political prisoners and servants to labor alongside African slaves. The harsh treatments condoned within the Acts mentioned earlier in this essay, underpinned by the severity of early sugar production, led to a forceful pushback "against violent overseers," from both Black and white servitude alike.[263] French voyager Beauchamp Plantagenet, visiting the island in 1648, observed a world, where he described, "rich men, [as] having sugar mils" and many hundreds Rebell Negro slaves [absconded] in the woods."[264] Based on the stringent laws passed by an assembly of rich men, as early as 1652, Ligon mentioned, that large numbers of indentured white servants conspired to "cut the throats of their masters," and ran away to "make themselves not only 'freemen,' but Masters of the Island." Many of the servants involved in that conspiracy were swiftly executed, as he noted. Ligon continued, with a more sympathetic tone of validation, stating that, "the root cause [of insurrection] grew from their sufferings" and the inability of some "to endure such slavery."[265] As a result, "several Irish servants and negroes [were] out in rebellion." Indentured servants, as Hilary Beckles affirms, like their African counterparts, were

---

[262] Jennifer L. Morgan, *Laboring Women: Reproduction and Gender in New World Slavery* (Philadelphia: University of Pennsylvania Press, 2004), 44.

[263] *[Acts and Statutes] of the Island of Barbados Made and Enacted since the Reducement of the Same, unto the Authority of the Common-Wealth of England / and Set Forth the Seventh Day of September, in the Year of Our Lord God 1652 ....* (London: Printed by Will. Bentley, 1654), 17, 28,81.

[264] Beauchamp Plantaganet, *A Description of the Province of New Albion: Preface* (London: James Moxon, 1650), 3.

[265] Ligon, *A True and Exact History*, 45–46.

"treated as chattel," and both groups steadfastly struggled against those conditions.[266]

Barbados was the birthplace of race in a class-gripped Atlantic World. Ultimately, as a response to the dangers invoked by all amalgamation of labor both Black and white, assemblies and their strategically "racialized edicts of division," beginning in seventeenth-century Barbados, spread throughout the Caribbean and beyond, including the early formed North American colonies, later planted firmly in South Carolina. In fact, by 1664, the newly established governor of the island of Jamaica, Sir Thomas Modyford (an acolyte of Oliver Cromwell himself), together with other "land-hungry" Barbadian elite, passed scarcely modified forms of both the Servant Act and the Slave Act of Barbados, maintaining a race-based "declaration of war" on what they defined as "outlying Spanish Negroes."[267] As Rugemer makes clear, Modyford, as "an agent for the newly formed ... Royal African Company in 1663," motivated by self-interest and profit, "brought with him to the new colony [of Jamaica] an intimate understanding of the effort to establish racial slavery."[268] As an example, by the time of Jamaica's Servant Act of 1681,[269] the assembly introduced, codified and adopted a somewhat new word, *white,* in place of the longtime

---

[266] Hilary McD. Beckles, "A 'Riotous and Unruly Lot': Irish Indentured Servants and Freemen in the English West Indies, 1644-1713," *The William and Mary Quarterly* 47, no. 4 (1990): 515–16.

[267] Barry Gaspar, "With a Rod of Iron: Barbados Slave Laws as a Model for Jamaica, South Carolina, and Antigua, 1661-1697," in *Crossing Boundaries: Comparative History of Black People in Diaspora*, ed. Darlene Clark Hine and Jaqueline McLeod (Bloomington: Indiana Univ. Press, 1999), 353.

[268] Rugemer, "The Development of Mastery," 443.

[269] "An Act of Regulating Servants (1681)," in *Acts of Assembly Passed in the Island of Jamaica; from 1681, to 1737, Inclusive* (London: Printed by J. Baskett, 1738), 2–5.

signifier of "Christian" - a change that elucidates the sustained efforts by the elite English of the Caribbean to clearly racialize, demarcate and justify the enslavement of Black bodies in a class tiered system of domination.

In conclusion, the rules put in place by the ruling class of Barbados and Jamaica unmistakably delineated their powers over a mass of human beings, in perpetual vassalage, defined as slaves. As argued, the foundations of racialized slavery which developed throughout the latter part of the seventeenth century, in Barbados and Jamaica, mutually and codependently, progressed toward a self-authorized legal system that was grounded in the "protection of property" and the privileges of the planter-elite - well into and throughout the eighteenth century. This essay's objective was to reveal the fact that constructs of race based on formulations of superiority were sown and birthed in the ruthless Atlantic Slave Trade and its dynamic Sugar Revolution. The elements of law, class, race, religion, and revolt, mentioned within this study, work cumulatively to expose why racialized enslavement occurred and who most benefited from it. In regard to matters of universal rights of humanity, including all creeds and races, when it comes to the relationship between possessors and the possessed, rulers and the ruled: The history of slavery teaches us that, "all human phenomena virtually require that oppression breed resistance, that exploitation be met by fight-back that compels the oppressor to acknowledge the humanity of the oppressed."[270] In the end, fighting fire with fire was the last and only resort left for the enslaved peoples of a darker hue in and throughout the Atlantic World; and, the saga of that struggle endures to this very day.

---

[270] Christopher Tomlins, "Enslaving: Facies Hippocratica," in *Freedom Bound: Law, Labor, and Civic Identity in Colonizing English America, 1580–1865* (Cambridge University Press, 2010), 507.

Chapter Nine

WHERE THE NEGROES ARE MASTERS: A BOOK REVIEW

Harvard University Press presents *Where the Negroes are Masters: An African Port in the Era of the Slave Trade,* by Randy J. Sparks. Cambridge, MA: 2014, 328 pages, $26.70.

In *Where the Negroes Are Masters,* historian Randy Sparks brings to the fore in detail the story of an eighteenth-century African Gold Coast slave-trading-port by the name of Annamaboe (situated in present-day Ghana). The author outlines, in elegant prose punctuated by historical evidence, the settlement's zealous profitmaking activity and its endemic brutality by revealing the lived practices of the commercial elite (both African and European alike), who lorded over and thrived upon a primitive capital accumulation brought forth by the vicious and insidious trafficking of human beings.

The point of this book, which reads like a historical novel, is to lay bare the "organized destruction" and/or "profit above all else" mentality and systemization that undergirded a mixed-race milieu and hitherto generally unknown multiracial class dynamic - which helped formulate the brutal Atlantic Slave Trade. Most readers will not only be shocked by the tales told, but also impressed by the sheer volume of supportive historical evidence provided - which can be described as up close and personal. As Sparks states in his introduction, "This book listens to those individual notes and seeks to understand the history of Annamaboe by focusing on the people of Africa ... [those] who lived, worked and traded there" (p.4). Delving deeper into the historical record, Sparks relies heavily on esteemed primary source collections like, *The English in West Africa, 1691–1699* edited by Robin Law; L. F. Rømer's, *A Reliable Account of the Coast of Guinea* (1760); and, the UK National Archives - just to name a few.

By way of the cultural, commercial, and personal encounters that were nurtured by profiteers and elites alike throughout locations typified by Annamaboe, this book brings forth a novel impression of the early modern Atlantic world. Furthermore, this study exposes the fact that far from being mere pieces moved on a chessboard by foreign powers, elite African men, and women (due to their distinctive negotiation skills) played a key strategic role in the intricately woven networks of the Atlantic Slave Trade – by examining how Annamaboe became the center of Atlantic commerce, Sparks throws the despair, greed, and grief of this slaving realm into stark relief.

The author's spotlight shines intently on a privileged class of African slave traders that were tied into, and benefited from, an intricate web of connections to their European counterparts. Within this complex multifaceted slave trade, Sparks focuses on a hitherto unknown character by the name of John Corrantee. Corrantee, as portrayed, stood above all others: an African nobleman at the center of slave commerce. As a fulcrum elevated above belligerent African slave extractions (amongst his coastal people the Fante and the hinterland Asante tribes), Corrantee was able to produce the valuable bodies necessary to appease his European business partners. As Paul Ocobock observes, "Through skillful, often devious, diplomatic, military, and commercial maneuvering, Corrantee brought prosperity and strategic importance to the

Fante of Annamaboe."[271] Clearly, Corrantee's life was inextricably intertwined with English slave profiteers.

Finally, *Where the Negroes Are Masters* is an important contribution to the study of slavery, yet, at the same time, the writing style is geared more toward a general audience rather than a scholastic one. Thus, the author could have provided a clearer definition of terms to assist students of interest. To assume that the Fante are universally well-known is a mistake; the point being: clarity of terminology is essential in history writing. In addition, there is some needless reiteration throughout the tale, the saga of an African prince (Corrantee's son William) with which the volume begins is repeated later in the book verbatim. A more careful proofreading would have remedied these shortcomings in what is otherwise a significant and thought-provoking work. Lastly, a further examination of how the establishment of an interracial class-stratified elite ideology directly influenced the vicious sociological and cultural norms developed later in the Americas would have been instructive to all.

---

[271] Paul Ocobock, "Where the Negroes Are Masters: An African Port in the Era of the Slave Trade," *Canadian Journal of History* 51, no. 3 (2016), 660.

Chapter Ten

PHILADELPHIA AND THE DARKSIDE OF LIBERTY: A DISSERTATION

PHILADELPHIA AND THE DARKSIDE OF LIBERTY

INTRODUCTION

This planned investigation, titled *Philadelphia and The Darkside of Liberty,* is a deliberate examination into the cultural, economic, and sociopolitical foundations which undergirded America's early colony and its newly birthed land of liberty's class-stratified slave society - combined with a closer look at the contradictions which laid within the notions and/or paradoxes of early American equality, freedom, race, and enslavement (commencing in the seventeenth-century). This proposed study therefore will contend that to appreciate the early interpretations of American political organization, it is essential to understand its beginnings – centering on the U.S. Constitution. This review will initially focus principally (however not exclusively) on the distinct influences of important personages such as James Madison, Thomas Jefferson, Alexander Hamilton, John Jay, Gouverneur Morris, and others - imbued within early American thought and thus influenced by renowned Enlightenment thinkers such as John Locke, David Hume, and Adam Smith - exemplified and exhibited in the celebrated Federalist Papers, with a specific and detailed focus on No.10;[272] additionally including

---

[272] James Madison, "Federalist Papers: Primary Documents in American History: Federalist No. 10," research guide, accessed August 27, 2023, https://guides.loc.gov/federalist-papers/text-1-10.

Jefferson's *Notes on Virginia,*[273] which will help to outline and undergird the key arguments put forth by this study.

Many of those notables that assembled in the city of Philadelphia in that historic year of 1787 were intent on framing a resilient centralized government that stood in accordance with Adam Smith's essential maxims which affirmed that "Civil government, so far as it is instituted for the security of property, is in reality instituted for the defense of the rich against the poor, or of those who have some property against those who have none at all;" contending that civil government, "grows up with the acquisition of valuable property."[274] Consequently, this analysis will challenge that long-held notion which has described early American thought and society as "egalitarian, free from [the] extreme want and wealth that characterized Europe."[275] In fact, as will be demonstrated throughout the work that follows, by an array of noted scholars and academics, this exploration will prove that property, class, and status played a significant, although perhaps not an exclusive, role in the development of that early colony and its nascent nation.

The intricacies of these contradictions will be examined in further detail throughout this study, arguing that, it is impossible to elude the fact that status, class, and race performed a major part in the views and doctrines woven within the principles and legal mechanisms formulated by those luminaries in that early republic. In fact, the following quote extracted from a letter written in 1786 by a French

---

[273] Thomas Jefferson, *Notes on the State of Virginia: An Annotated Edition, Notes on the State of Virginia* (Yale University Press, 2022).

[274] Adam Smith, *An Inquiry into the Nature and Causes of the Wealth of Nations* (London: G. Routledge, 1893), 556–60.

[275] Michael Parenti, *Democracy for the Few*, 8th ed (Boston: Thomson-Wadsworth, 2008), 40.

diplomat (positioned as the chargé d'affaires), in communiqué with his government, leading up to the Constitutional Convention of 1787, helps to delineate the top-down attitudes and devices engineered by the men historically known as the "Framers:"

> Although there are no nobles in America, there is a class of men denominated "gentlemen." ... Almost all of them dread the efforts of the people to despoil them of their possessions, and, moreover, they are creditors, and therefore interested in strengthening the government and watching over the execution of the law.... The majority of them being merchants, it is for their interest to establish the credit of the United States in Europe on a solid foundation by the exact payment of debts, and to grant to Congress powers extensive enough to compel the people to contribute for this purpose.[276]

As supported, evidenced, and argued by famed bottom-up historians like Michael Parenti, Charles A. Beard, Michael J. Klarman, and others, the concepts of class and ownership and their European legacy greatly contributed to the initial composition of that early American dominion and its proprietorship stratum. In fact, as Professor Parenti demonstrates, "from colonial times onward, 'men of influence' received vast land grants from the [English] crown and presided over estates that bespoke an impressive munificence." Parenti also reveals the stark differentials woven within the colonial class structure through exposing the fact that, "By 1700, three-fourths of the acreage in New

---

[276] Louis Otto quoted in Herbert Aptheker, *Early Years of the Republic: From the End of the Revolution to the First Administration of Washington (1783-1793)* (New York: International Publishers, 1976), 41.

York belonged to fewer than a dozen persons." And, beyond that, "In the interior of Virginia, seven individuals owned 1.7 million acres," exhibiting a structuralized formulation of wealth concentration from early on. In the run-up to the American Revolution, some twenty-seven years prior to the Continental Congress taking place in that celebrated year of 1787, Professor Parenti additionally notes that, "By 1760, [some] fewer than five hundred men in five colonial cities controlled most of the commerce, shipping, banking, mining, and manufacturing on the eastern seaboard." Again, Parenti brings to the fore, a clear demarcation between the few and the many, property ownership and capital accumulation in that newly formed land of "equality," which will be explored and surveyed in further detail within this work.[277]

Chapter One of this dissertation will do a deep dive, in part, by focusing on documentary evidence penned by the "Framers" themselves. In addition to that, this work will seek to challenge existing historiographical debates, as noted, by displaying both the negative and positive legacy left by the men that articulated the U.S. Constitution in the city of Philadelphia in that momentous year of 1787. Furthermore, a major theoretical element of this retrospective will be working with, and challenging, the classifications and clashes within the so-called American ideals of Independence, Liberty, and Equality through studying an array of viewpoints from historical masterworks by Gordon S. Wood, Woody Holton, and others as mentioned below. Some of the topics brought forth within this research will include Chapter One, "An

---

[277] Michael Parenti, *Democracy for the Few*, 40. Sourcing the works of Sidney H. Aronson, *Status and Kinship in the Higher Civil Service: Standards of Selection in the Administrations of John Adams, Thomas Jefferson, and Andrew Jackson* (Cambridge, Mass: Harvard University Press, 1964); Daniel M. Friedenberg, *Life, Liberty, and the Pursuit of Land: The Plunder of Early America* (Buffalo, N.Y: Prometheus Books, 1992).

American Paradox: The Marriage of Liberty, Slavery and Freedom." Chapter Two, "Cui Bono - Who Benefitted Most from the Categorical Constructs of Race and Class in Early America?" And, finally, in Chapter Three, this work will take a cogent look at "The Atomization of the Powerless and the Sins of Democracy," historically from antiquity and beyond, by reflecting upon the judgments, attitudes, and viewpoints, from a class perspective, of the privileged faction of men that forged that early nation's crucial founding doctrines and documents. Again, these chapters above mentioned will take a thorough look at the varying constructs of race and class throughout the American experience from the Eighteenth, Nineteenth, and early part of the Twentieth centuries, focusing on cui bono, that is, who benefitted most from those racialized constructs of division and how those benefits negatively affected those societies at large socially, politically, and culturally.

Specifically, the chapters summarized above will bring together the importance of understanding just how class, ownership, and status, per race, position, and wealth demarcated the early American experience within governmental and societal structures, rules, and regulations from 1787 forward - surveying the uniqueness of the U.S. Constitution (both pro and con) along with its Amendments (known as the Bill of Rights) will help provide a nuanced understanding of both said document and the men that formulated it. Which later impacted social movements and social discord from abolitionism to civil rights. This study will deliver not just a structuralized economic and political viewpoint, but a humanistic perspective. Moreover, this research will incorporate historical and scientific classics by such noted scholars as Edmund S. Morgan, Edward E. Baptist, Barbara J. Fields; and Nancy Isenberg - just to name a few. The foundations of racial divisions mentioned above were clearly measured by 16th-century English theorist and statesman Francis Bacon when he penned, "The Idols of the Tribe have their foundation in human nature itself, and in the tribe or race of men."[278] As determined, Bacon defined racism as an innate element of human nature. Hence, this study will challenge that hypothesis, in part, by arguing that divisions of race within the human condition are social constructs that ultimately benefit those that exercise those dictates.

---

[278] Francis Bacon, *The Philosophical Works of Francis Bacon, with Prefaces and Notes by the Late Robert Leslie Ellis, Together with English Translations of the Principal Latin Pieces*, ed. James Spedding, vol. 4 (London: Longman & co., 1861), 64.

1

THE PARADOX OF EARLY AMERICAN FREEDOM

What were the underlying moral and ideological contradictions woven within that newly birthed land of freedom's class-stratified slave society?

We believe we understand what class is, that being, an economic social division shaped by affluence and privilege versus want and neglect. "The problem is that popular American history is most commonly told, [or] dramatized, without much reference to the existence of social classes." The story, in the main, is taught and/or conveyed as a tale of American exceptionalism - as if the early American colonies, and their break with Great Britain, somehow miraculously transformed the constraints of class structuralism - resulting in a greater realization of "enriched possibility." This conception of America was galvanized by the men that formulated its constitution in the city of Philadelphia in that momentous year of 1787 with great elegance - an image of how a modern nation "might prove itself revolutionary in terms of social mobility in a world traditionally dominated by monarchy and fixed aristocracy." America's most beloved myths are at once encouraging and devastating: "All men are created equal,"[279] for example, which excluded Indigenous Peoples and African Americans, penned by renowned American statesman and philosopher Thomas Jefferson in his landmark Declaration of Independence written in 1776 - was effectively employed as a maxim to delineate, as historian Nancy Isenberg presents, "the promise of America's open spaces and united people's moral self-regard in distinguishing themselves from a host of hopeless societies abroad," but the tale is much darker, more troublesome and abundantly more nuanced than that.[280]

An elite colonial land-grabbing class, from early on, in that fledgling America, contrived its own attitudes and perspectives - those which served it best. After settlement, starting as early as the seventeenth century, colonial outposts exploited their unfree labor: European indentured servants, African slaves, Native Americans, and their offspring - describing such expendable classes as "human waste."[281] When it comes to an early settler-colonial mentality of not only conquest but profitability as an exemplar, "Coined land," is the term that Benjamin Franklin (noted Eighteenth Century political philosopher, scientist, and diplomat) used to refer to, or celebrate, the intrinsic monetary value woven within the then brutal land acquisition and/or theft from the Indigenous Native American population at the time – appropriated land which was later "privatized and commodified" in the hands of

---

[279] "Declaration of Independence: A Transcription," America's Founding Documents, National Archives, accessed March 22, 2024, https://www.archives.gov/founding-docs/declaration-transcript.

[280] Nancy G. Isenberg, *White Trash: The 400-Year Untold History of Class in America* (New York, New York: Penguin Books, 2017), 1.

[281] Isenberg, 1.

venture capitalists, described as "European colonists."[282]
These attitudes of hierarchy over "the people out of doors," as
those eminent luminaries that gathered in Philadelphia later
referred to them were long held. A phrase, according to noted
Professor of History Benjamin Irvin, that was largely defined
to incorporate not only "the working poor" that clamored in
the streets of Philadelphia during the Convention of 1787, but
all peoples who were disenfranchised by that newly formed
Continental Congress, "including women, Native Americans,
African Americans, and the working poor."[283] In fact, as
Isenberg demonstrates, notions of superiority from the upper
crust of that early society toward, "The poor, [or waste
people], did not disappear, [on the contrary], by the early
eighteenth century they [the lower classes] were seen as a
permanent breed."[284] That is, a taxonomical classification
viewed through how one physically appeared, grounded in
their class and conduct, came to the fore; and, this prejudicial
manner of classifying and/or categorizing bottom-up human
struggle or failure took hold in the United States for centuries
to come - which will be further explored within subsequent
chapters.

These unfavorable top-down class attitudes toward the
poor or "waste people" emanated from what was known at the
time as the mother country, that is, England itself - where as
early as the 1500s and 1600s, America was not viewed as an
"Eden of opportunity," but rather a "giant rubbish heap," that
could be converted and cultivated into productive estates, on
behalf of wealthy landowners through the unloading of

---

[282] David McNally, *Blood and Money: War, Slavery, Finance,
and Empire* (Chicago, Illinois: Haymarket Books, 2020), 178.

[283] Benjamin Irvin, *Clothed in Robes of Sovereignty: The
Continental Congress and the People Out of Doors* (New York:
Oxford University Press, 2011), 1–18.

[284] Isenberg, *White Trash*, 1.

England's poor and destitute - who would be used to develop that far-off wasteland. Again, as Isenberg contends, "the idle poor [or] dregs of society, were to be sent thither simply to throw down manure and die in a vacuous muck." That is, before it became celebrated as the fabled "City on a Hill,"[285] auspiciously described by John Winthrop (English Puritan lawyer and then governor), in his well-known sermon of 1630, to what was then the early settlement of the Massachusetts Bay Colony, "America was [seen] in the eyes of sixteenth-century adventurers [and English elites alike] as a foul, weedy wilderness – a 'sink-hole' [perfectly] suited to [work, profit and lord over] 'ill-bred commoners,'"[286] clearly defining top-down class distinctions from early on.

Returning to those eminent American men that later devised the doctrines and documents which conceived of a "new nation" built on individual liberty and freedom, under further examination, begs the question: "Freedom for whom and for what?" This study will delve deeper into who those men were and how their overall attitudes toward the general populous as far as class, education, rank, and proprietorship, eventually led to a decisive result known as the U.S. Constitution. To appreciate the U.S. political and economic structure, it is essential to understand its original formulation, starting with said constitution. Those dignitaries that gathered in Philadelphia in 1787 were intent on framing a strong centralized government in adherence with (what they believed to be Scottish economist and theorist) Adam Smith's fundamental dicta and/or revelations, which stated that government was "instituted for the defense of the rich against

---

[285] John Winthrop, "A Modell of Christian Charity, 1630," in *Collections of the Massachusetts Historical Society*, 3rd Series (Boston, 1838), 7:31-48, https://history.hanover.edu/texts/winthmod.html.

[286] Isenberg, *White Trash*, 3.

the poor" and "grows up with the acquisition of valuable property."[287] As Political Scientist and author, Robert Ovetz argues below, the mechanisms and/or devices designed and implemented within the U.S. Constitution were contrived from the outset to thwart any and all democratic control. Equally noted, the Framers' brilliance was in formulating a virtually unalterable system which offered through clever slogans like "We the People" an assurance of participation within the constructs of a Republic, all the while permitting "a few to hand-pick some representatives," whilst the majority thus surrendered "the power of self-governance." The U.S., still to this day, lauds itself as a "Democracy," yet, from the outset, as argued, that illustrious landmark charter mentioned was nefariously intended to "impede democratic control of government" all the while foiling "democratic control of the economy."[288]

Under careful observation, no section of the U.S. Constitution is more misconstrued and misinterpreted than its Preamble. Moreover, the term, "We the People," for example was, and still is to this day, deliberately employed as a rhetorical device in the form of a "philosophical aspiration," separating it from the dry legalese that compose most of the rest of the charter. This, perhaps, is why the Preamble . has grasped the attention of the common everyday citizen. It embodies the hopes and values of ordinary people, cunningly expressing what they would ideally like the Constitution to achieve in practice – even though in truth it does something distinctively different. In fact, if we survey the meaning of the doctrines found within the Preamble, we find a set of material relations dating back to the 1700s which were brilliantly

---

[287] Smith, *Wealth of Nations*, 556–60.

[288] Robert Ovetz, *We the Elites: Why the US Constitution Serves the Few* (London: Pluto Press, 2022), 2–3.

devised to deliberately constrain economic and political democracy:[289]

Figure 1: The original handwritten Preamble to the U.S. Constitution on permanent display at the National Archives.

> We the People of the United States, in Order to form a more perfect Union, establish Justice, insure domestic Tranquility, provide for the common defense, promote the general Welfare, secure the Blessings of Liberty to ourselves and our Posterity, do ordain and establish this Constitution for the United States of America.[290]

The "Blessings of Liberty" run amiss. Again, those "Framers," or group of elite men that gathered in Philadelphia for that historic event in 1787 ideally utilized the inclusive language of "We the People," . while at the same time, implementing a complex structural formulation which would stave off the will of the common people at every turn. The fifty-five of the seventy-four delegates that showed up on the scene, were, in fact, a cohort indistinguishable from themselves as "wealthy white men" of whom only a small number were not rich (but nevertheless affluent). They viewed themselves as "the People," who would not only be provided liberties under that newly devised constitution, but also

---

[289] Ovetz, 41.

[290] "The Constitution of the United States," National Archives, accessed September 3, 2023, https://www.archives.gov/founding-docs/constitution.

offered themselves the power to control the authority within that newly formed centralized government.[291]

Figure 2: The Framers working out the concept of "We the People" by Tom Meyer.

By bringing the term "insure domestic Tranquility" to the fore, an early American top-down class paradigm is made evident by those men of property historically known as the "Framers." The U.S. Constitution was the result of the repercussions of the American Revolution and decades of class conflict from within. Cogent warnings provided by not only Jefferson's Declaration of Independence,[292] which cautioned against "convulsions within" and "exciting domestic insurrections amongst us," but also forewarnings offered by the man considered "the father of that newly formed nation," George Washington. In the following statements to the run-up of the Constitutional Convention of 1787, written in correspondence to his then erstwhile comrade-in-arms and chief of artillery, General Henry Knox, George Washington (supreme commander of the American revolutionary colonial forces and hero par excellence)

---

[291] Steve Fraser and Gary Gerstle, *Ruling America: A History of Wealth and Power in a Democracy* (Cambridge: Harvard University Press, 2009), 40.

[292] "Declaration of Independence: A Transcription."

projected clear class distinctions, fears and/or biases which lie at the heart of this study, "There are combustibles in every state, to which a spark might set fire."[293] Hence, as Professor of Law, Jennifer Nedelsky asserts, what General Washington believed was necessary was a statutory formulation of control, instituted and devised by the upper crust of society, in the shape of a constitution, "to contain the threat of the people rather than to embrace their participation and their competence,"[294] or else, as stated in a second letter to Knox, the eminent General warned, "If government shrinks, or is unable to enforce its laws ... anarchy & confusion must prevail – and every thing will be turned topsy turvey,"[295] demonstrating an elite fear most pronounced.

Figure 3: George Washington (1732-1799), Supreme Commander of the American Revolution and First President of the United States.

---

[293] "From George Washington to Henry Knox," December 26, 1786, Founders Online, National Archives, http://founders.archives.gov/documents/Washington/04-04-02-0409.

[294] Jennifer Nedelsky, *Private Property, and the Limits of American Constitutionalism: The Madisonian Framework and Its Legacy*, Paperback ed., (Chicago: Univ. of Chicago Press, 1994), 159.

[295] "From George Washington to Henry Knox," February 3, 1787, Founders Online, National Archives, https://founders.archives.gov/documents/Washington/04-05-02-0006.

A good exemplar of a "spark that set fire," which struck fear in the hearts of that elite class of men assembled in Philadelphia, is famously known as Shays' Rebellion (August 29, 1786 to February 1787), led by former American army officer and son of Irish Immigrants, Daniel Shays, which culminated in a bottom-up armed revolt that took place in Western Massachusetts and Worcester, in response to a debt crisis imposed upon, in large part, the common citizenry; and, in opposition to the state government's increased efforts to collect taxes on both individuals and their trades – as a remediation for outstanding war debt. The rebellion was eventually put down by Colonial Army forces sent there by George Washington himself – staving off the voice of the people, in that newly formed land of liberty. What "Tranquility" actually meant, as established by the Framers, was a centralized government formulated within the constitution, with the ability to halt and/or suppress conflict or unrest that threatened "the established order and governance of the elite."[296] Shays' Rebellion in combination with the possibility of slave uprisings and native resistance offered the justification for creating, and later expanding, a domestic military force as penned into the Charter by Gouverneur Morris (1752 – 1816), American political leader and contributor to the Preamble outlined above. Morris cleverly emphasized the necessity for a general fiscal "contribution to the common defense" on behalf of his class interests, warning of the possible dangers of both "internal insurrections and external invasions" as outlined in detail in

---

[296] Gregory H Nobles, "Historians Extend the Reach of the American Revolution," in *Whose American Revolution Was It? Historians Interpret the Founding*, ed. Alfred Fabian Young and Gregory H. Nobles (New York: New York University Press, 2011), 213.

Article I Section 8 of the U.S. Constitution.[297] In summary, by centralizing a military power within a national charter, "the elites got their own protection force against the possibility of the majority's 'popular despotism'" as described by Washington himself – thwarting any and all popular resistance to elite rule. In fact, by 1791, just four years after the Constitutional Congress met in the city of Philadelphia, that newly formed nation's military force tripled its cost and increased its number of troops by fivefold.[298]

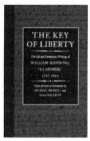

Figure 4: The Key of Liberty: The Life and Democratic Writings of William Manning, "a Laborer," 1747–1814

In challenging that ideal of promoting "the general Welfare," within a class paradigm, William Manning, (1747 – 1814) American Revolutionary soldier, farmer, and novelist, was one of the few voices at the Constitutional Convention that stood up and pushed back against the elite coup that was evidently taking place. After having fought in the Revolutionary War, as a common foot soldier, he began to believe that his military service and sacrifice carried little weight with the elites that surrounded him. He also delineated the fact that those measures which reflected Alexander

---

[297] "The Constitution of the United States."

[298] Richard H. Kohn, *Eagle and Sword: The Federalists and the Creation of the Military Establishment in America, 1783-1802* (New York: Free Press, 1975), 80, 95, 120.

Hamilton, George Washington, and (the first President of the Continental Congress) John Jay's views, and policies, created a poisonous atmosphere, ideology, and division between the "Few and the Many." William Manning feared that by locking "the people out of doors," out of government, the Founders were implementing measures such as Hamilton's economic vision for that newly formed nation "at the expense of the common farmer and laborer."[299] When it came to Shays' Rebellion, for example, his views were commensurate with those of the uprising, but not with their methods of armed resistance. Based on his staunch democratic values, he called upon the common man to forcefully use new organizational tactics by directly petitioning the government to redress grievances. Manning understood the economic divisions as implemented.[300] In 1798, he authored his most celebrated work, *The Key of Liberty*, in which he displayed what he believed to be the objectives of the "Few" – which were to "distress and force the Many" into being financially dependent on them, "generating a sustained cycle of dependence." Manning argued that the only chance for the "Many" was to choose those leaders that would battle for those with lesser economic and political authority.[301] What Manning understood so well was that those early colonial financial interests defined their own class "influence and benefits" as "the general Welfare" which was, in his view, in diametrical opposition to much of the population.

---

[299] William Manning, *The Key of Liberty: The Life and Democratic Writings of William Manning, "a Laborer," 1747-1814*, ed. Michael Merrill and Sean Wilentz, The John Harvard Library (Cambridge, Mass: Harvard University Press, 1993), 113.

[300] Manning, 164–66.

[301] Manning, 162.

Figure 5: Alexander Hamilton (1757-1804), the First Secretary of the Treasury from 1789 to 1795 during George Washington's presidency.

Alexander Hamilton's celebrated financial plan alluded to above, put that early nation on a trajectory of economic growth, through a concentration of wealth in the form of property and holdings which would serve his class best, "...so capital [as] a resource remains untouched."[302] Hamilton delivered an innovative and audacious scheme in both his First and Second Reports on the Further Provision Necessary for Establishing Public Credit issued on 13 December 1790. Again, on behalf of his class interests, that newly devised federal government would purchase all state arrears at full cost – using its general tax base. Hamilton understood that such an act would considerably augment the legitimacy of that newly formed centralized government. To raise money to pay off its debts, the government would issue security bonds to rich landowners and wealthy stakeholders who could afford them, providing huge profits for those invested when the time arrived for that recently formed Federal government to pay off its debts.[303] Charles Beard, Columbia University historian and

---

[302] Alexander Hamilton, "Final Version: First Report on the Further Provision Necessary for Establishing Public Credit," December 13, 1790, Founders Online, National Archives, http://founders.archives.gov/documents/Hamilton/01-07-02-0227-0003.

[303] Alexander Hamilton, "Final Version of the Second Report on the Further Provision Necessary for Establishing Public Credit (Report on a National Bank)," December 13, 1790, Founders Online, National Archives, http://founders.archives.gov/documents/Hamilton/01-07-02-0229-0003.

author, in his famed book, *An Economic Interpretation of The Constitution of The United States*, succinctly outlines Hamilton's class bias woven within his strategy per taxation, "[d]irect taxes may be laid, but resort to this form of taxation is rendered practically impossible, save on extraordinary occasions, by the provision that 'they [taxes] must be apportioned according to population' – so that numbers cannot transfer the burden to accumulated wealth"[304] - revealing a significant economic top-down class preference and formulation of control from the outset. Beard summarizes as such, "The Constitution was essentially an economic document based upon the concept that the fundamental private rights of property are anterior to government and morally beyond the reach of popular majorities."[305] Given the United States' long history of top-down class biases and bottom-up class struggle, to be further explored within this research, Beard provides a cogent groundwork.

Figure 6: James Madison (1751-1836), Father of the U.S. Constitution and Fourth President of the United States.

---

[304] Charles Austin Beard, *An Economic Interpretation of the Constitution of the United States* (Anodos Books, 2018), 88.

[305] Beard, 164.

James Madison, elite intellectual and Statesman, was and is traditionally proclaimed as the "Father of the Constitution" for his crucial role in planning and fostering the Constitution of the United States and later its Bill of Rights. For many of the Framers, with Madison in the lead, the Articles of Confederation (previously formulated on November 15, 1777, and effectuated on March 1, 1781) were a nefarious compact among the 13 states of the United States, previously the Thirteen Colonies of Great Britain, which operated as the nation's first framework of government establishing each individual State as "Free and Independent" - eloquently encouraged and outlined in Thomas Jefferson's Declaration of Independence.[306] From a class vantage point, the phrase "establish Justice" as devised by Madison within the Preamble above, meant in an idealistic sense, that the government would apply the rule of law impartially and consistently to all, irrespective of one's station in society. But, in fact, the expression, "establish Justice," explicitly points to the Framers' "intent to tip the balance of power back in favor of the elites."[307] Notably, by early 1783, in his famed "Notes on Debates in Congress Memo" dated January 28th, 1783, some four years prior to the ratification of the U.S. Constitution on December 12th, 1787, Madison had well-defined what "justice" had meant to him and his cohorts by asserting that, "the establishment of permanent & adequate funds [in the form of a general taxation] to operate … throughout the U. States is indispensably necessary for doing complete justice to the Creditors of the U.S., for restoring public credit, & for providing for the future exigencies of …

---

[306] "Declaration of Independence: A Transcription."

[307] Ovetz, *We the Elites*, 44.

war."[308] For Madison, as argued by eminent Professor of History Woody Holton, "establishing Justice" envisioned doing what some of the States were reluctant and/or incapable of achieving – that being, the payment of debts for the elites by "safeguarding their property" whether it be slave, land, or financial.[309]

How class and race maintained supremacy. In essence, the cleverly devised Three-fifths Compromise outlined in Article 1, Section 2, Clause 3 of the U.S. Constitution, conceived by Madison, not only preserved, and reinforced the atrocity of slavery, but it also made stronger "the power of property" produced by the capitalization of all human labor. The minority checks embedded in the constitutional power of taxation ultimately prevented all types of what the Framers referred to as "leveling," that being a fair and equal redistribution of wealth and resources amongst the general population.[310] In doing so, the constitution serves in perpetuity to protect wealth from what the Framers feared most: "economic democracy."[311] Unambiguously, the Three-fifths clause established that three out of every five enslaved persons were counted, on behalf of their owners, when deciding a state's total populace per representation and legislation. Hence, before the Civil War, the Three-fifths clause gave disproportionate weight to slave states, specifically slave ownership, in the House of Representatives.

---

[308] James Madison, "Notes on Debates" (January 28, 1783), Founders Online, National Archives, https://founders.archives.gov/documents/Madison/01-06-02-0037.

[309] Woody Holton, *Unruly Americans and the Origins of the Constitution*, First Edition (New York: Hill and Wang, 2008), 87–88.

[310] "The Constitution of the United States."

[311] Ovetz, *We the Elites*, 96.

A final element written within the Preamble of the U.S. Constitution worth further mention is the famed idiom "secure the Blessings of Liberty to Ourselves and Our Posterity," a phrase that concisely encompasses the opinions of that band of elites, that amassed in Philadelphia, known as "the Framers" and their historical and material view of the possession of "Private Property" – greatly influenced and inspired by English Enlightenment philosopher and physician John Locke (1632-1704). Locke, in his famed *The Two Treatises of Civil Government*, argued that the law of nature obliged all human beings not to harm "the life, the liberty, health, limb, or goods of another," defined as "Natural Rights."[312] As a result, the Framers (most of whom were large landowners) were intent on designing a centralized government that would singularly protect and defend "private property." The U.S. Constitution fosters this by placing a collection of roadblocks and/or obstacles in the way of majority demands for "economic democracy" – what, on numerous occasions, James Madison himself described as an oppression, enslavement and/or tyranny of the majority.[313] In a land without Nobles, Madison declared that "the Senate ought to come from, and represent, the wealth of the nation."[314] With Madison's compatriot John Dickinson of

---

[312] John Locke, *Two Treatises on Civil Government* (London: G. Routledge and Sons, 1884), 160.

[313] "From James Madison to James Monroe," October 5, 1786, Founders Online, National Archives, http://founders.archives.gov/documents/Madison/01-09-02-0054; "To Thomas Jefferson from James Madison," October 24, 1787, Founders Online, National Archives, http://founders.archives.gov/documents/Jefferson/01-12-02-0274; Madison, "Research Guides."

[314] James Madison quoted in Michael J. Klarman, *The Framers' Coup: The Making of the United States Constitution* (New York, NY: Oxford University Press, 2016), 210.

Delaware in full accord, proclaiming that the Senate should be comprised of those that are, "distinguished for their rank in life and their weight of property, and bearing as strong a likeness to the British House of Lords as possible."[315] Additionally, Pierce Butler, wealthy land-owning South Carolinian, stood in complete agreement confirming that the Senate was, "the aristocratic part of our government."[316] Those elite men, as members of that continental congress, largely on their own behalf, cleverly formulated "a plethora of opportunities to issue a minority veto of any changes by law, regulation, or court rulings," that might menace their property ownership.[317] In essence, that charter known as the U.S. Constitution was brilliantly constructed to ensure an elite control and privilege that would last for "Posterity" - forever unchanged and unchangeable.

There is a wealth of evidence, as demonstrated, that the U.S. Constitution was originally designed and implemented not to facilitate meaningful bottom-up systemic change, but to ultimately avert anything that does not serve the benefits of the propertied class. Let us keep in mind that meaningful change from below has always been hard-fought, but not impossible. It took roughly seventy-eight years from 1787; and, a Civil War which lasted from 1861 to 1865, culminating in the loss of nearly 620,000 lives to officially abolish slavery under Amendment XIII (ratified on December 6th, 1865).[318] Until then, human bondage was a long held and integral form of property ownership within the United States – to be further examined within this work. Reflecting succinctly on the underlying class interests during and prior to the ratification

---

[315] John Dickinson quoted in Klarman, 210.

[316] Pierce Butler quoted in Klarman, 210.

[317] Ovetz, *We the Elites*, 53.

[318] "The Constitution of the United States."

of the U.S. Constitution, two indispensable statements, concerning "human nature," from two essential minds, per class, which undergird the views here summarized, are as follows: Benjamin Franklin keenly observed that any assemblage of men, no matter how gifted, bring with them "all their prejudices, their passions, their errors of opinion, their local interest and their selfish views."[319] Which stood ironically in accordance with Adam Smith's, "All for ourselves, and nothing for other people, seems, in every age of the world, to have been the vile maxim of the masters of mankind,"[320] which demonstrates Smith's historical view per an innate class perspective of wealth concentration.

---

[319] Max Farrand, ed., *The Records of the Federal Convention of 1787* (New Haven: Yale University Press, 1911), 642.

[320] Smith, *Wealth of Nations*, 342.

2

CUI BONO – Who Benefitted Most from the Categorical Constructs of Race and Class?

The year 1776 is a deceptive starting point when it comes to the ideologies of American freedom and liberty. Independence from Great Britain did not expunge the British class arrangement long embraced by colonial elites that undergirded a social system of division which promulgated "entrenched beliefs about poverty and the willful exploitation of human labor." An unfavored view of African slaves and poor whites widely thought of as "waste and/or rubbish," remained a long-held social construct which served American elites well into the modern era.[321] From the outset, when it came to class dynamics, no one understood the manipulative power of faction and discord sown amongst the masses better than James Madison himself as boldly outlined in Federalist #10. The danger, Madison argued on behalf of his class interests, was not faction itself, but the escalation of "a majority faction" grounded in that "most common and durable source" of conflict: the "unequal distribution of property."[322] In that widely celebrated land of "democracy," Madison revealed not only his class biases anathema to the concept, but his fear of the very idea: "When a majority is included in a faction," it could use democracy, "to sacrifice to its ruling

---

[321] Isenberg, *White Trash*, 14.
[322] Madison, "Research Guides."

passion or interest the public good and the rights of other citizens" – that is, the privileges of the propertied class.[323] To his credit, from early on, James Madison laid out clear class distinctions, partialities, and fears woven within that newly formulated American social stratum – which are essential to this study. Within Federalist #10, Madison brilliantly devised a strategy of division which would protect elite interests by suppressing the economic menace of a majoritarian class faction through the encouragement of as many divisions within the populous as possible. Hence, as he outlined, the "greater variety of parties and interests [within class, race, gender, or religion] ... make it less probable that a majority of the whole will have common motive."[324] Ironically, faction was problematic as stated, yet, at the same time, paradoxically, according to James Madison, more of it was the answer.

From the outset of the American experience, as outlined in his masterwork, *American Slavery, American Freedom,* Edmond S. Morgan, Yale Professor of History, makes evident the elite class interests and/or dynamics that fortified the use of clever rhetorical devices, such as "freedom and liberty" upon the general populous - all the while devilishly using the cruelty of slavery as a unifying force. During his visit to that early America, an astute English diplomat by the name of Sir Augustus John Foster, serving in Washington during Jefferson's presidency (1801-1809), keenly observed, "[Elite] Virginians above all, seem committed to reducing all [white] men to an equal footing." Foster observed, "owners of slaves, among themselves, are all for keeping down every kind of superiority"; and he recognized this pretension of equality used upon the masses as a powerful manipulative tactic.

---

[323] Madison.

[324] Madison.

Virginians, he argued, "can profess an unbounded love of liberty and of democracy in consequence of the mass of the people, who in other countries might become mobs, being there nearly altogether composed of their own Negro slaves…."[325] In that ruthless slave society, as Morgan reveals, "Slaves did not become leveling mobs, because their owners would see to it that they had no chance to. The apostrophes to equality were not addressed to them."[326] In clarification, he adds:

> …because Virginia's labor force was composed mainly of slaves, who had been isolated by race and removed from the political equation, the remaining free [white] laborers and tenant farmers were too few in number to constitute a serious threat to the superiority of the [elite white] men who assured them of their equality.[327]

The ancient Roman concept of Divide and Conquer, which dates to Julius Caesar himself, was effectively implemented by Virginia's elite propertied class through the skillful use of cooptation. Virginia's yeoman class comprised of small land-owning farmers were made to believe that they shared "a common identity" with those "men of better sorts," simply due to the fact that neither was a slave – hence, both were alike in not being slaves.[328] Ironically, in the mindset of those early American elites that viewed themselves as the founders of a republic, largely inspired by Oliver Cromwell's

---

[325] Augustus John Foster, *Jeffersonian America: Notes on the United States of America, Collected in the Years 1805-6-7 and 1-12* (San Marino, Calif.: Huntington Library, 1954), 163, 307.

[326] Edmund S. Morgan, *American Slavery, American Freedom: The Ordeal of Colonial Virginia* (New York: Norton, 1995), 380.

[327] Morgan, 380.

[328] Morgan, 381.

Common-wealth and the pushing off of monarchy, slavery occupied a critical, if not indeterminate position: it was thought of as a principal evil which free men sought to avoid for society in general through the usurpation of monarchies and the establishment of republics. But, at the same time, it was also viewed as the solution to one of society's most pressing problems, "the problem of the poor." Elite Virginians could move beyond English republicanism, "partly because they had solved the problem: they achieved a society in which most of the poor were enslaved."[329] In truth, contempt for the poor permeated the age. John Locke, English philosopher and physician (1632-1704), considered one of the most essential of Enlightenment thinkers, commonly read, discussed, and admired by early American elites, famously wrote a classic defense of the right of revolution in his *Two Treatises of Civil Government* published in 1689 – yet he did not extend that right to the poor. [330] In fact, in his proposals for workhouses and/or "working schools," outlined in his *Essay on the Poor Law,* published in 1687, the children of the [English] poor would "learn labor," and nothing but labor, from a very young age, stopping short of enslavement - though it would require a certain alteration of mind to recognize the distinction.[331] That said, those astute men that assembled in the city of Philadelphia in 1787 took their inspiration from Locke very seriously.

Hamilton and Madison were in absolute accord with Locke's views per property and ownership, that being, "Government has no other end but the preservation of

---

[329] Morgan, 381.

[330] Locke, *Two Treatises on Civil Government*, 169–75.

[331] John Locke, "An Essay on the Poor Law," in *Political Essays*, ed. Mark Goldie, Transferred to digital print, Cambridge Texts in the History of Political Thought (Cambridge: Cambridge University Press, 2007), 190–91.

property."[332] Consequently, the U.S. Constitution was designed to both govern the population through limiting its capacity to self-govern; and by protecting all forms of property ownership including the enslavement of human beings. Hence, as historian David Waldstreicher (expert in early American political and cultural history) presents, the Constitution was devised not only to safeguard slavery as a separate economic system, but as integral to the basic right of what he describes as the "power over other people and property (including people who were property)."[333] As a result, the tensions and/or rivalries that resided in that newly formed nation, which would eventually lead to a bloody Civil War, were not over quantities of land possession between the North and the South, but more focused on how many slaves resided in each. To his credit, Madison presciently admitted as such:

> [T]he States were divided into different interests not by their difference of size … but principally from the effects of their having or not having slaves. These two causes concurred in forming the great division of interests in the U. States. It did not lie between the large & small States: It lay between the Northern & Southern.[334]

Slavery was considered insidious by some, and yet fundamental to those that profited from it, both North and South. In fact, John Rutledge, esteemed Governor of South Carolina during the Revolution; and delegate to the

---

[332] Locke, *Two Treatises on Civil Government*, 239–40.

[333] David Waldstreicher, *Slavery's Constitution: From Revolution to Ratification* (New York: Hill and Wang, 2009), 14.

[334] James Madison, "Rule of Representation in the Senate," June 30, 1787, Founders Online, National Archives, https://founders.archives.gov/documents/Madison/01-10-02-0050.

Constitutional Convention, spoke on behalf of the Southern planters' class by supporting slavery, of which, Charles Cotesworth Pinckney also of South Carolina, stood in full agreement. Both men implored their fellow delegates to recognize their common interests in preserving slavery from which they "stood to profit," not only from selling slave-produced goods, but from carrying the slaves on their ships[335] – hence, they argued, stood a long-held alliance between Northern "personality" (that is, financial holdings) and "that particular form of property" (slavery) which dominated the South.[336] Slaves were long held the most valuable asset in the country. By 1860, the total value of all the slaves in America was estimated at the equivalent of $4 billion, more than double the value of the South's entire farmland valued at $1.92 billion, four times the total currency in circulation at $435.4 million, and twenty times the value of all the precious metals (gold and silver) then in circulation at $228.3 million.[337] Thus, at the time and thereafter, North American slavery was not just a national or sectional asset, but a global one. As a result of the promise of monetary benefits and values produced by enslaved peoples, "the Framers," in defense of their own interests, collectively devised a system of fail-safe mechanisms to protect their most cherished resource: human vassalage.[338] Moreover, in addition to the

---

[335] James Madison, "Madison Debates," August 22, 1787, Yale Law School, The Avalon Project, https://avalon.law.yale.edu/18th_century/debates_822.asp.

[336] Staughton Lynd, *Class Conflict, Slavery and the United States Constitution: Ten Essays* (Westport, Conn: Greenwood Pr, 1980), 14.

[337] Roxanne Dunbar-Ortiz, *Loaded: A Disarming History of the Second Amendment* (San Francisco: City Lights Books, 2017), 65.

[338] Michael J. Klarman, *The Framers' Coup: The Making of the United States Constitution* (New York, NY: Oxford University Press, 2016), 294.

Three-Fifths Clause described above, the Constitution contained several safeguards with a clear objective of maintaining the vile system as it was. The Foreign Slave Trade Clause as outlined in Article 1; Section 9 of that charter known as the U.S. Constitution stated that Congress could not prohibit the "importation of persons" prior to 1808 – which cleverly excluded the term "slave."[339] The intention of said clause, was not to stave off slavery, but was implemented to maintain, if not inflate, the monetary value of those persons already in captivity - when it came to their sale and transport to other slave states outside of Virginia. The Fugitive Slave Clause as written in Article IV, Section 2, Clause 3, was clearly devised to protect elite proprietorship over individuals forcefully ensconced in a system of chattel slavery:

> No Person held to Service or Labour in one State, under the Laws thereof, escaping into another, shall, in Consequence of any Law or Regulation therein, be discharged from such Service or Labour, but shall be delivered up on Claim of the Party to whom such Service or Labour may be due.[340]

This Clause, not nullified until the Thirteenth Amendment's abolition of slavery, considered it "a right" on the part of a slaveholder, to retrieve an enslaved individual who had fled to another state. Finally, as esteemed University of Chicago Professor, Paul Finkelman, contends, the ban on congressional export taxes adamantly argued for by those elite men that gather in Philadelphia, was, for the most part, a concession to southern planters whose slaves primarily

---

[339] "The Constitution of the United States."
[340] "The Constitution of the United States."

produced agricultural goods for export.[341] Clearly demonstrating and demarcating an upper-class bias based on ownership, race, and wealth from the outset.

How elite capture worked in early America – diversity was implemented and utilized as a ruling class ideology. Privileged landowners, specifically Virginians, being "men of letters," as they would have thought of themselves, understood very well that all white men were not created equal, especially when it came to property and what they referred to as "virtue," a much admired "elite attribute" which can be traced back to Aristotle himself, in his classic work, *Nicomachean Ethics*, who defined the only life worth living as "a life of leisure" – that is a life of study and freedom for the few which rested on the labor of slaves and proprietorship.[342] As thus revealed, the material forces and benefits which dictated southern elites to see Negroes, mulattoes, and Indians as one, also "dictated that they see large and small planters as one." Consequently, racism became an essential, if unacknowledged, ingredient woven within that "republican ideology" that enabled Virginians to not only design, but to "lead the nation," for generations to come. An important question thus addressed: Was the ideological vision of "a nation of equals" flawed from the very beginning by the evident contempt, exhibited, toward both poor whites and enslaved blacks? And beyond that, to be further explored within the final chapter of this research project: Are there still elements of colonial Virginia, ideologically, ethnically, and socially, woven within America

---

[341] Paul Finkelman, "Slavery in the United States: Person or Property," in *The Legal Understanding of Slavery: From the Historical to the Contemporary*, ed. Jean Allain (Oxford: Oxford Univ. Press, 2012), 118.

[342] Aristotle, *Nicomachean Ethics*, trans. W. D. Ross, 2009, https://classics.mit.edu/Aristotle/nicomachaen.html.

today? More than a century after Lee's surrender at Appomattox (on April 9th, 1865) - those questions per race and class still linger....[343]

As Edward E. Baptist, Professor of History at Cornell University, makes clear in his epic work, *The Half Has Never Been Told, Slavery and The Making of American Capitalism,* attitudes toward race and race superiority in America long remained. By the late nineteenth and early twentieth century, America's first generation of professional historians, he argues, "were justifying the exclusion of Jim Crow and disfranchisement" by telling a story about the nation's past of slavery and civil war that seemed to confirm, for many white Americans, that "white supremacy was just and necessary." In fact, Baptist proclaims that racism had not only become culturally accepted, but historically and socially grounded within a form of "race science" to be further explored in the final chapter of this study. He states that by the latter part of the nineteenth century, "for many white Americans, science had proven that people of African descent [if not the poor in general] were intellectually inferior and congenitally prone to criminality." As a result, he argues, that that cohort of racist whites in [Jim Crow] America, "looked wistfully to [the] past when African Americans had been governed with whips and chains." Confirming the fact that class, race, and racism have long been integral parts of America's long and difficult history.[344]

American capitalism, land, cotton, slaves, and profit: by the early nineteenth century, the U.S. Banking system was fundamental when it came to entrepreneurial revenue

---

[343] Morgan, *American Slavery, American Freedom*, 386–87.

[344] Edward E. Baptist, *The Half Has Never Been Told: Slavery and the Making of American Capitalism*, Paperback edition (New York: Basic Books, 2016), xviii–xix.

development in the form of land acquisition, cotton production, and slave labor. Bank lending became the key ingredient that propelled slave owners to greater heights of wealth accumulation, "Enslavers benefited from bank-induced stability and steady credit expansion." The more slave purchases that U.S. Banks would finance, the more cotton enslavers could produce, "and cotton [at the time] was the world's most widely traded product." As mentioned, in this newly devised system of capital, lending, and borrowing, cotton was an essential resource in an unending global market. So, the more cotton slaves produced, the more cotton enslavers would sell, and thus the more profit they would make. In fact, "owning more slaves enabled planters to repay debts, take profits, and gain property that could be [used as] collateral for even more borrowing."[345] Early U.S. Capitalism not just undergirded, but bolstered and expanded the harsh and inhumane system of slavery as such, "Lending to the South's cotton economy was an investment not just in the world's most widely traded commodity, but also in a set of producers who had shown a consistent ability to increase their productivity and revenue."[346] Said differently, American slave owners, throughout the late eighteenth and early nineteenth century, had the "cash flow to pay back their debts." And, the debts of slave owners were secure, given the fact that they had "a lot of valuable collateral." In fact, as argued by a number of economic historians, enslavers, by mid-century had in their possession the largest pool of collateral in the United States at the time, 4 million slaves worth over $3 billion, as "the

---

[345] Baptist, 244–45.

[346] Baptist, 245.

aggregate value of all slave property."[347] These values embedded themselves in a global system of investment through slave commodification which benefitted mostly the upper crust of society in both the U.S. and the U.K., "this meant that investors around the world would share in revenues made by 'hands in the field.'" Even though at the time, and to its credit, "Britain was liberating the slaves of its empire," British banks could still sell, to a wealthy investor, a completely commodified human being in the form of a slave – not as a specific individual, but as a holding or part of a collective investment venture "made from the income of thousands of slaves." [348]

Furthermore, as mentioned, the fact that popularly elected governments repeatedly sustained such bond schemes, on both sides of the Atlantic, was therefore not only insidious by its very nature, but at the same time remarkable. Popular abolitionist movements were springing up from one side to the other, and demanding abolition across the board. Beyond that, in the United States, there were many elements of class recognition in the form of an "intensely democratic frontier electorate" of both slaves and poor whites that saw banks as "machines designed to channel financial benefits and economic governing power to the unelected elite."[349] By mid-century, the rift and divisions between the North and the South became catastrophic in the form of a bloody Civil War. It took a poor boy from a dirt-floor cabin in Kentucky named Abraham Lincoln, who rose to the prominence of lawyer and

---

[347] Steven Deyle, "The Domestic Slave Trade in America: The Lifeblood of the Southern Slave System," in *The Chattel Principle: Internal Slave Trades in the Americas*, ed. Walter Johnson and Gilder Lehrman Center for the Study of Slavery, Resistance, and Abolition (New Haven, CT: Yale University Press, 2004), 95.

[348] Baptist, *The Half Has Never Been Told*, 248.

[349] Baptist, 248.

statesman becoming the 16th President of the United States, to write and implement the Emancipation Proclamation brought forth on January 1st, 1863. As President, Abraham Lincoln issued that historic decree, which served not only as a direct challenge to "property ownership," in the form of human bondage, but a direct assault on the lucrative southern slaveocracy as the nation approached its third year of bloody civil war. The proclamation declared "that all persons held as slaves within the rebellious states are, and henceforward shall be free."[350] Although Lincoln's, contribution has been much contested to this day, by historians both Black and white alike, the fact remains that, his efforts as already presented, were undoubtedly a more active and direct support for the freedom of African slaves than those of all the fifteen previous presidents before him combined – The Emancipation Proclamation would prove to be the most important executive order ever issued by an American president, offering the possibility of freedom to an enslaved people held in a giant dungeon that was the confederacy.[351] Even though there are those historians that argue that the Proclamation was incomplete due to the fact that it "excluded the enslaved not only in Union-held territories such as western Virginia, but also southern Louisiana" where there were pro-Union factions that were trying not to be antagonistic toward local whites who were hell-bent on maintaining the status quo.[352]

But facts speak for themselves, Abraham Lincoln had been working diligently to persuade the political class in the

---

[350] Abraham Lincoln, "The Emancipation Proclamation, 1863," January 1, 1863, https://www.archives.gov/exhibits/american_originals_iv/sections/nonjavatext_emancipation.html.

[351] James M. McPherson, "Who Freed the Slaves?," *Proceedings of the American Philosophical Society* 139, no. 1 (1995): 1–10.

[352] Baptist, *The Half Has Never Been Told*, 400–401.

border states that were loyal to the Union to agree to a "gradual or compensated" emancipation plan – pushing back against the benefactors of the race and class divide. Even though some within the border states refused to give in and held out for permanent slavery, by April 1862, because of Lincoln's tenacious efforts, Congress passed legislation "freeing – in return for payments to enslavers totaling $1 million – all 3,000 people enslaved in the District of Columbia, Maryland, Delaware and Kentucky." After the Union army's victory at the battle of Antietam, Lincoln felt "he could move more decisively" against the institution of slavery and hence released that historic executive order which he had written months earlier as outlined above.[353] Undoubtedly, again, the Emancipation Proclamation offered for the first time in American history the unquestioned possibility of freedom to a long-held and enslaved people that were seized in a giant open-air prison which was the American South. The Emancipation did unbar the door. Next, enslaved Africans, due to their own agency, forced it wide open.[354]

As an exemplar of that heartfelt commitment, stood Frederick Douglass (1818 – 1895), former slave in his home state of Maryland, who rose to become a historic social reformer, abolitionist, writer, orator, and statesman. Lincoln was the first U.S. President in a long line, to invite an eminent African American intellectual, such as, Frederick Douglass to the White House to discuss the wonton discrimination within the military ranks cast upon African American men. That well-known meeting between Lincoln and Douglass took place in August 1863, two years after the start of the war on April 12, 1861. Douglass tenaciously argued for the enlistment of Black soldiers in the Union Army based largely

---

[353] Baptist, 400.
[354] Baptist, 401.

on his legendary speech delivered at the National Hall in Philadelphia (on July 6, 1863), a month prior, entitled "the Promotion of Colored Enlistments," outlined in the well-known publication *The Liberator,* that same month. Where Douglass stated:

> Let the black man get upon his person the brass letters US … a musket on his shoulder, and bullets in his pocket, and there is no power on earth or under the earth which can deny that he has earned the right of citizenship in the United States.[355]

Douglass presented the same argument to Lincoln, that "Black men in Blue" would not only swell the ranks of the Union Army but would elevate those former slaves to the status of free men of honor – shifting the course of American history.[356] Lincoln took decisive action, per Douglass' request, enlisting nearly 200,000 battle-ready African Americans, understanding that without those Black soldiers, there would be no Union. As a result, Douglass wholeheartedly endorsed the President for his coming reelection on November 8, 1864. "The enlistment of blacks into the Union Army was part of Lincoln's evolving policy on slavery and race."[357] Ultimately, he paid the price. On April 14, 1865, the 16th President of the United States was brutally slain by an assassin's bullet for his valiant efforts against the racist slavocracy known as the Confederacy - *Lincoln died at*

---

[355] "SPEECH OF FREDERICK DOUGLASS: Delivered at a Mass Meeting Held at National Hall, Philadelphia, July 6, 1863, for the Promotion of Colored Enlistments," *Liberator (1831-1865),* American Periodicals, 33, no. 30 (July 24, 1863): 118.

[356] David W. Blight, *Frederick Douglass: Prophet of Freedom* (New York: Simon & Schuster, 2020), 409–10.

[357] John T. Hubbell, "Abraham Lincoln and the Recruitment of Black Soldiers," *Papers of the Abraham Lincoln Association* 2, no. 1 (1980).

7:22 a.m. on April 15, 1865.[358] The Civil War ultimately nullified the barbarity of slavery, which was later codified in the 13th Amendment of the U.S. Constitution, true, yet prejudicial elements of both race and class remained a fixture in American society for decades to come....

In the latter part of the nineteenth century, the coalescing or coming together from a class perspective of the lower ranks in the American South, later revealed itself in the formulation of the "Colored Farmers' Alliance," which stood as a direct threat to the established southern regime leading to a brutal and repressive racialized crackdown in the form of the Ku Klux Klan and the implementation of an oppressive social order known as Jim Crow - to be further explored within this study.

---

[358] "Lincoln's Death," Ford's Theatre, accessed July 16, 2024, https://fords.org/lincolns-assassination/lincolns-death/.

3

THE ATOMIZATION OF THE POWERLESS AND THE SINS OF DEMOCRACY

Finally, as alluded to, the appellation and/or utilization of the term "race" was seldom employed by Europeans prior to the fifteen-hundreds. If the word was used at all, it was used to identify factions of people with a group connection or kinship. Over the proceeding centuries, the evolution of the term "race," that came to comprise skin color, levels of intelligence and/or phenotypes, was in large part a European construct – which served to undergird a strategy of division amongst the masses that helped to maintain a stratified class structure with "elite white land-owning men" placed firmly at the top of the social-ladder in that newly birthed land of "freedom" called America.

As succinctly stated by David Roediger, esteemed Professor of American history at the University of Kansas, who has taught and written numerous books focused on race and class in the United States, "The world got along without race for the overwhelming majority of its history. The U.S. has never been without it."[359] Nothing could be further from the truth. As outlined in previous chapters, American society

---

[359] David R. Roediger, *How Race Survived US History: From Settlement and Slavery to the Eclipse of Post-Racialism*, Paperback edition (London New York: Verso, 2019), XII.

uniquely and legalistically formulated the notion of "race" early on to not only justify, but support its new economic system of capitalism, which rested in large part, if not exclusively, upon the exploitation of forced labor – that is, the brutal enslavement and demoralization of African peoples. To understand how the development of race and its bastardized twin "racism" were fundamentally and structurally bound to early American culture and society we must first survey the extant history of how the notions of race, ethnocentrism, white supremacy, and anti-blackness came to exist.

The ideas that undergirded the notions of "race, a class-stratified stratified slave society, as we recognize them today, were birthed and developed together within the earliest formation of the United States; and were intertwined and enmeshed in the phraseologies of "slave" and "white." The terms "slave," "white," and "race" began to be utilized by elite Europeans in the sixteenth century and they imported these hypotheses of hierarchy with them to the colonized lands of North America. That said, originally, the terms did not hold the same weight they have today. However, due to the economic needs and development of that early American society, the terms mentioned would transform to encompass new racialized ideas and meanings which served the upper class best. The European Enlightenment, defined as, "an intellectual movement of the 17th and 18th centuries in which ideas concerning god, reason, nature, and humanity were synthesized into a worldview that gained wide assent in the West and that instigated revolutionary developments in art, philosophy, and politics,"[360] would come to underpin and contribute to racialized perceptions which argued that, "white

---

[360] Brian Duignan, "Enlightenment," in *Encyclopedia Britannica*, July 29, 2024, https://www.britannica.com/event/Enlightenment-European-history.

people were inherently smarter, more capable, and more human than nonwhite people - became accepted worldwide." In fact, from an early American perspective, "This [mode] of categorization of people became the justification for European colonization and subsequent enslavement of people from Africa."[361] To be further surveyed.

As Paul Kivel, noted American author, social-justice educator and activist, brings to the fore, the terms "white" or "whiteness," historically, from a British/Anglo-American perspective, served to underpin class distinctions and justify exploitation through human bondage by providing profit-accumulation to a distinct ownership class, "Whiteness is [historically] a constantly shifting boundary separating those who are entitled to have privileges from those whose exploitation and vulnerability to violence is justified by their not being white."[362] Where and how did it begin? The conception of "whiteness" did not exist until roughly 1613 or so, when Anglo-Saxon forces, later known as the English, first "encountered and contrasted themselves" with the Indigenous populations of the East Indies - through their cruel and rapacious colonial pursuits – later justifying, and bolstering, a collective cultural sense of racial superiority. Up and until that point, roughly the 1550s to the 1600s, within Anglo-Saxon society, "whiteness" was used to set forth clear class signifiers.

In fact, the word "white" was utilized exclusively to "describe elite English women," because the whiteness of

---

[361] "Historical Foundations of Race," National Museum of African American History and Culture, accessed July 30, 2024, https://nmaahc.si.edu/learn/talking-about-race/topics/historical-foundations-race.

[362] Paul Kivel, *Uprooting Racism: How White People Can Work for Racial Justice* (Gabriola Islands, BC: New Society Publ, 1996), 127.

their skin indicated that they were individuals of "high social standing" who did not labor "out of doors." That said, conversely, throughout that same period, the appellation of "white" did not apply to elite English men, due to the stigmatizing notion that a man who would not leave his home to work was "unproductive, sick and/or lazy." As the concept of who was white and who was not began to grow, "whiteness" gained in popularity within the Anglo-American sphere, for example, "the number of people that considered themselves white would grow" as a collective pushback against people of color due to immigration and eventual emancipation.[363] These social constructs centered around race accomplished their nefarious goals – thus, unifying early colonists of European descent under the rubric of "white," and hence, marginalizing, stigmatizing and dispossessing native populations – all the while permanently enslaving most African-descended people for generations. As acclaimed African American Professor, Ruth Wilson Gilmore (director of the Center for Place, Culture, and Politics at CUNY) contends concerning America's base history, "Capitalism requires inequality and racism enshrines it...."[364] A revelatory statement by John Jay (1745-1829, the first Chief Justice of the United States and signer of the U.S. Constitution) helps make evident, from a class perspective, the entrenched values of those early American elites toward their newly proclaimed democracy, "The people who own the country ought to govern

[363] "Historical Foundations of Race."

[364] Ruth Wilson Gilmore, "The Worrying State of the Anti-Prison Movement," in *Abolition Geography: Essays towards Liberation*, ed. Brenna Bhandar and Albero Toscano (Brooklyn: Verso, 2022), 451.

it!"[365] The preceding two quotes help to summarize and clarify the top-down legal and societal mechanisms embedded within that early American social stratum which linger to this day.

The social status and hence the nomenclature of "slave" have been with mankind for millennia. Historically, a slave was one who was classified as quasi-sub-human, derived from a lower lineage; and forced to toil for the benefit of another of higher standing. We can find the phraseology of slave throughout the ancient world and within early writings from Egypt, the Hebrew Bible, Greece, and Rome, as well as later periods. In fact, Aristotle (384 to 322 BC, famed polymath, and philosopher) succinctly clarified, from his privileged vantage-point, the social standing and value of personages classified as slaves - which would endure for epochs to come. From the legendary logician's point of view, a slave was defined as, "one who is a human being belonging by nature not to himself [or herself] but to another is by nature a slave." Aristotle further described a slave as, "a human being belongs to another if, in spite of being human, he [or she] is a possession; and as a possession, is [simply a tool for labor] having a separate existence."[366] Clarifying the fact that in the known world prior to Columbus' famed voyage, in the late 15th century, opening the floodgates of European colonial theft, pillage, and domination, historical notions of Western hierarchy and supremacy were commonplace. As European Enlightenment ideals such as, "the natural rights of man," aforementioned, became ubiquitous amongst early American

---

[365] Quoted in Richard Hofstadter, *The American Political Tradition: And the Men Who Made It*, Vol Vintage Books, 1989, 15–16.

[366] Aristotle, *Politics*, trans. Harris Rackham, Loeb Classical Library (Cambridge, Mass: Harvard University Press, 1944), 1.5 1254a13-18, https://catalog.perseus.org/catalog/urn:cts:greekLit:tlg0086.tlg035. perseus-eng1.

colonial elites throughout the 18th century, "equality" became the new modus operandi which galvanized whites over and above all others. Hence, by classifying human beings by "race," a new method of hierarchy was established based on what many at the time considered "science" to be further explored. As the principles of the Enlightenment penetrated the colonies of North America forming the basis for their early "democracy," those same values paradoxically undergirded the most vicious kind of subjugation – chattel slavery.[367]

A significant codified shift took place in colonial America within one of its most prosperous slave domains known as Virginia. Under the tutelage and guidance of the then Governor Sir William Berkeley (1605-1677), wealthy planter and slave owner, the House of Burgesses (the first self-proclaimed "representative government" in that early British colony) included a coterie of councilors hand-chosen by the governor to enact a law of hereditary slavery - which would economically serve their elite planter class interests. The English common law, known as, *Partus Sequitur Patrem,* traditionally held that, "the offspring would follow the condition ... of the father."[368] But after a historic legal challenge brought by Elizabeth Key, an enslaved, bi-racial woman who sued for her freedom and won, in 1656, on the basis that her father was white – elite white Virginians understood that a shift in the law was not only necessary, but essential, if they were to maintain and/or increase their wealth through human bondage in the form of "property ownership." Consequently, the new 1662 law, *Partus Sequitur Ventrem,* diverged from English common law, in that it proclaimed that

---

[367] "Historical Foundations of Race."

[368] James H. Kettner, *The Development of American Citizenship, 1608 - 1870* (Chapel Hill, N.C: Univ. of North Carolina Press, 1984), 14–15.

the status of the mother, free or slave, determined the status of her offspring in perpetuity.[369] Thus, African women were subjugated to the ranking of "breeders," that would serve to produce more offspring categorized as slaves, whether biracial or not, and hence more profit for the ruling class. Enlightenment values ensconced in a rudimentary "race science," by famed early Americans, would also help to solidify a systematized racialized hierarchy for decades to come.[370]

Figure 7: Thomas Jefferson (1743-1826), Diplomat, Son of the Enlightenment, Planter, Lawyer, Philosopher, Primary Author of the Declaration of Independence and Third President of the United States.

Thomas Jefferson is famed to be one of the most quintessential characters in the formulation of America's early Republic, along with James Madison and others, severing foreign rule and developing a new independent nation, substantiated on the Enlightenment principles of "Life,

---

[369] Tarter Brent, "Elizabeth Key (Fl. 1655-1660) Biography," in *Dictionary of Virginia Biography* (Library of Virginia, 2019), Available at: https://www.lva.virginia.gov/public/dvb/bio.asp?b=Key_Elizabeth_fl_1655-1660.

[370] Richard H. Popkin, "The Philosophical Basis of Eighteenth-Century Racism," in *Racism in the Eighteenth Century*, ed. Harold E. Pagliaro (Cleveland: Case Western Reserve University Press, 1973), 246.

Liberty and the pursuit of Happiness,"[371] based largely on John Locke's *Two Treatises of Government*, which argued that true "freedom" is defined by one's singular control over their holdings and/or estates, i.e., property.[372] But the most basest question which still lingers, within America's long and twisted historical tragedy of early conquest and domination, which must be probed, is, "freedom for whom and for what?" Jefferson, that complex and enigmatic son of Enlightenment thought, both in science and sociological principles, clearly demarcated and endorsed a racialized societal structure that undergirded a system of hierarchy in which white colonists and their European legacy were considered far superior to all others – simplified notions woven within an early race science which would endure through time and memorial. Throughout his lifetime, race was defined by phenotype (or the look of human beings), physical characteristics which "appended physical traits [or idiosyncrasies] defined as 'slave-like' [were attributed] to those enslaved."[373] As Karen and Barbara Fields, two noted African American scholars, point out, Jefferson became convinced that a forced separation of people delineated by skin color was the only solution; that "the very people white Americans had lived with for over 160 years as slaves would be, after emancipation, too different for white people to live with any longer."[374] In fact, he suggested that if slaves were to be freed they should be promptly deported,

---

[371] "Declaration of Independence: A Transcription."

[372] Locke, *Two Treatises on Civil Government*.

[373] Stephen Jay Gould, *The Mismeasure of Man* (New York: Norton, 1981), 132–35, 149–51.

[374] Karen E. Fields and Barbara Jeanne Fields, *Racecraft: The Soul of Inequality in American Life* (London: Verso, 2014), 18.

their lost labor to be best supplied "through the importation of white laborers."[375]

Jefferson unabashedly qualified his racialized views when writing, "I advance it therefore as a suspicion only that the blacks, whether originally a distinct race, or made distinct by time and circumstances, are inferior to the whites in the endowments both of body and mind."[376] John Locke and Thomas Jefferson stood in agreement, philosophically, when it came to the superiority versus inferiority of selected "races," underpinning a racialized stratification within early colonial thought that helped to culturalize a race-based hierarchy in that newly formed "land of freedom," known as the United States. These arguments of hierarchy which spread throughout the European mindset within that early colonial era, aided and abetted, "the dispossession of Native Americans" and "the enslavements of Africans" during that golden era of revolution.[377] In his historic manuscript known as, *Notes on the State of Virginia*, Jefferson outlined in detail his Enlightenment-inspired racialized interpretations of European superiority, demarcating what he believed to be a "scientific view" of the varying gradations of human beings based on race:

> Comparing them [both blacks and whites] by their faculties of memory, reason, and imagination, it appears to me, that in memory they are equal to the whites; in reason much inferior … and that in imagination they are dull, tasteless, and anomalous. But never yet could I find that a black has uttered a

---

[375] Thomas Jefferson, *Notes on the State of Virginia*, ed. William Harwood Peden (Chapel Hill, NC: Univ. of North Carolina Press, 1995), 137–38.

[376] Jefferson, 143.

[377] "Historical Foundations of Race."

thought above the level of plain narration; never see even an elementary trait, of painting or sculpture.[378]

Ironically, given the complexity of the man, in response to a critic who opposed his views as presented above, Jefferson confessed that even if blacks were inferior to whites, "it would not justify their enslavement."[379] Hence, to his credit, he admitted and/or recognized the strangeness and/or irony of his own position when it came to Enlightenment constructs of race and their structural consequences.[380] Again, from early on, racialized notions of superiority versus inferiority served the American planter class best, by cleverly embedding perceptions of hierarchy or white preeminence, they were able to suppress that which they feared most - which was the unification or coming together of a mass of lower classes comprising both enslaved Africans and poor whites. The historic incident which, served as an exemplar, sending shockwaves through that propertied class of early colonial America was notably Bacon's Rebellion of 1676.

Nathaniel Bacon (1647-1676) elite Virginian, born and educated in England, member of the governor's Council and close friend of Sir William Berkeley then colonial Governor - led a bottom-up rebellion which sent tremors through the upper classes of that newly birthed slave society, known as, Virginia - still considered one of the most foundational events of early American history. The colonial elite were threatened on all sides, as made evident by Governor Berkeley's revelation, "The Poore Endebted Discontented and Armed" would, he feared, use this opportunity to "plunder the

---

[378] Jefferson, *Notes on the State of Virginia*, 1995, 139.

[379] "Thomas Jefferson to Henri Gregoire, February 25, 1809" (Correspondence, February 25, 1809), Available at: https://www.loc.gov/resource/mtj1.043_0836_0836/?st=text.

[380] Fields and Fields, *Racecraft*, 18.

Country" and seize the property of the elite planters.[381] Bacon, "who was no leveler," was cleverly able to formulate a coalition (or unification), on behalf of his class interests, which included poor white indentured servants, free and enslaved Africans, to push back against any and all encroachments by native inhabitants which included the Appomattox and Susquehannock indigenous tribes of the region, in order to cease their lands and enrich himself and his class even further, insisting that, "the country must defend itself 'against all Indians in general for that they were all Enemies.'"[382] Some one hundred years later, in his acclaimed paradox of liberty known as the *Declaration of Independence*, Thomas Jefferson, obviously influenced by Bacon's racialized frame of thought, referred to the indigenous Native American peoples as nothing more than, "merciless Indian savages."[383] Hence, the native populations of that early America were collectively used as "scapegoats," to enlarge the land holdings and wealth of the propertied class. From early on, the United States' nascent form of Capitalism became dependent upon exploitative low-cost labor, "especially that of those considered nonwhite," but also that of "the poor in general, including women and children – black and white alike."[384] Ironically, by the 1850s, antislavery sentiment grew even more intense amongst the masses, largely spurred on by white Southerner's aggressive attempts to maintain the societal structure as such through political dominance and the spread of that "peculiar institution,"

---

[381] Sir William Berkeley quoted in Stephen Saunders Webb, *1676, the End of American Independence* (New York: Knopf, 1984), 16.

[382] Nathaniel Bacon quoted in Morgan, *American Slavery, American Freedom*, 255.

[383] "Declaration of Independence: A Transcription."

[384] "Historical Foundations of Race."

known as slavery to newly pilfered lands.[385] In turn, the very idea of the possibility of any and all "lower class unity," or a coming together of poor white indentured servants and African slaves as a militant force rising up against an entrenched planter class, brought forth a racialized culturalization grounded upon racial difference, racial hierarchy, and racial enmity, "a pattern that those statesmen and politicians of a later age would have found [politically useful and] familiar."[386] In fact, right through to the end of the 19th century, post-Civil War and *Reconstruction era* (1865-1877), any form of lower-class unity in America stood as a direct threat to the established order of things throughout the nation as a whole; and especially throughout the South - most notably in the form of the *Colored Farmers' Alliance* and the South's reactionary implementation of a brutal social-order of domination and control known as *Jim Crow*.

Figure 8: Abraham Lincoln (1809-1865), American Lawyer, Statesman and Politician. Sixteenth President of the United States and Author of the Emancipation Proclamation.

Although historically contentious, Abraham Lincoln's primary goal within his Reconstruction scheme was to reunite a fractured nation after a bloody and costly Civil War. Through which, Lincoln's objective was to reestablish the

---

[385] "Historical Foundations of Race."

[386] Morgan, *American Slavery, American Freedom*, 250–70.

union and transfigure that implacable Southern society. His plan was also stridently committed to enforcing progressive legislation driven by the abolition of slavery. In fact, Lincoln directed Senator Edwin Morgan, chair of the National Union Executive Committee, to put in place a constitutional amendment abolishing slavery. And Morgan did just that, in his famed speech before the National Convention on May 30, 1864, demanding the "utter and complete extirpation of slavery" via such an amendment.[387] Beyond the Emancipation Proclamation, Abraham Lincoln was the first President in American history to call forth an amendment to the U.S. Constitution abolishing the long-held institution of chattel slavery. For the first time, President Lincoln demanded the eventual passage of the *Thirteenth Amendment Section 1 (ratified on December 6, 1865)*, which mandated that, "Neither slavery nor involuntary servitude, except as a punishment for crime whereof the party shall have been duly convicted, shall exist within the United States, or any place subject to their jurisdiction."[388] Defining it as "a fitting, and necessary conclusion" to the war effort that would make permanent the joining of the causes of "Liberty and Union."[389] Lincoln's sweeping Reconstruction agenda was a fight for freedom, requiring the South to adhere to a new constitution that would implicitly include black suffrage through the ratification of the *Fourteenth Amendment Section 1*, ratified after his death on July 9, 1868, which for the first time in American history, declared:

---

[387] Eric Foner, *The Fiery Trial: Abraham Lincoln and American Slavery*, 1st ed (New York: W. W. Norton, 2010), 298–99.

[388] "The Constitution of the United States."

[389] Roy P. Basler, ed., *The Collected Works of Abraham Lincoln*, vol. VII (New Brunswick, N.J.: Rutgers University Press, c1953-55), 380.

All persons [meaning black and white alike]
born or naturalized in the United States and subject
to the jurisdiction thereof, are citizens of the United
States and of the State wherein they reside. No State
shall make or enforce any law which shall abridge
the privileges or immunities of citizens of the
United States; nor shall any State deprive any
person of life, liberty, or property, without due
process of law; nor deny to any person within its
jurisdiction the equal protection of the laws.[390]

Abraham Lincoln, the Great Emancipator, saw his
Reconstruction struggles above all as, "an adjunct of the war
effort – a way of undermining the Confederacy, rallying
southern white Unionists, and securing emancipation,"[391] for
which he paid the ultimate price. From early on, internecine
rivalry, or infighting, within the Republican Party from those
labeled as "the Radicals," led to a push-back against certain
elements of Lincoln's strategy mentioned above - arguing that
Reconstruction should be postponed until after the war, "as
outlined in the Wade-Davis Bill of 1864, which clearly
envisioned, as a requirement, that a majority of southern
whites take an oath of loyalty," to the United States; and that
the federal government should by necessity, "attempt to
ensure basic justice to emancipated slaves." A point at which,
"equality before the law," not "black suffrage," as Lincoln had
suggested, was an essential factor for many of the Republicans
in Congress at the time.[392] As a result of Lincoln's efforts in
taking away the productive forces of labor within the South,
and in turn, the diminishment of property, wealth, and
political power of the elite southern planter class, a nefarious

---

[390] "The Constitution of the United States."

[391] Foner, *The Fiery Trial*, 302.

[392] Foner, 302.

conspiracy to murder the President was hatched and executed by southern loyalist and assassin John Wilks Booth, on April 14, 1865, while the President sat accompanied by his wife, Mary, watching a play titled, *Our American Cousin,* at Ford's Theater in Washington, D.C. – oddly, the assassin was able to gain access to the theater, enter the Presidential Booth, and shoot and kill the President of the United States. Lincoln's body was carried to the nearby Petersen House, where he passed away at 7:22 a.m., the following morning. At his bedside, Secretary of War Edwin M. Stanton famously remarked, "Now he belongs to the ages."[393] Reflecting upon not only the uniqueness of the man, but his tremendous contributions to those American ideals of "Liberty and Freedom." Emphasizing the fact that the Emancipation of Africans from forced labor; and the abolishment of chattel slavery, through a stroke of his pen, uniquely placed Abraham Lincoln in the pantheon of historical renown.

That said, throughout the end of the 19th Century, the road ahead per class relations for African Americans and poor whites alike, especially in the South, would be a hard and arduous one of top-down control and division. Reactionary as they were, as argued, Southern elites would forcefully implement doctrines of superiority, separation, and control that would crush and/or punish any form of lower-class unity which threatened their power and influence over the majority. This reaction would become most evident in the racialized militant form of the *Ku Klux Klan;* and later the structural control and dominance of an imposed social order known as

---

[393] "Timeline: Assassination of President Abraham Lincoln," in *Library of Congress*, Articles and Essays, Digital Collections, accessed August 28, 2024, https://www.loc.gov/collections/abraham-lincoln-papers/articles-and-essays/assassination-of-president-abraham-lincoln/timeline/.

Jim Crow, which would orchestrate the groundwork for a deepening racial divide.

The *Colored Farmers' Alliance,* formulated in the 1870s, still stands as a historical model of class unity amongst the poor, both Black and white alike, which galvanized southern elites in a top-down belligerent class war to protect their interests. The *Alliance* was created, "when an agricultural depression hit the South around 1870 and poor farmers began to organize themselves into radical multiracial political groups"[394] – which stood as a direct threat to upper-class Southern dominance and their wealth accumulation. Years earlier by 1865, that elite militancy revealed itself in the form of the *Ku Klux Klan* (a violent and racist, hate-filled supremacist terror organization) that, "extended into almost every southern state by 1870 and became a vehicle for white southern resistance to the Republican Party's Reconstruction-era policies aimed at establishing political and economic equality for Black Americans."[395] *Klan* members devised a subversive crusade of coercion and brutal violence directed at Black and white Republican leadership. Even though the U.S. Congress had successfully pushed through regulations intended to mitigate *Klan* extremism, the *KKK* viewed its main goal as the "reinstatement of white governance and supremacy throughout the Southlands in the 1870s and beyond," made most evident through Democratic victories within state legislatures across the South.[396] *Jim Crow* was the

---

[394] Helen Losse, "Colored Farmers' Alliance," in *Encyclopedia of North Carolina,* ed. William S. Powell (Chapel Hill, NC: The University of North Carolina Press, 2006), Available at: https://www.ncpedia.org/colored-farmers-alliance.

[395] History.com Editors, "Ku Klux Klan: Origin, Members & Facts," History, April 20, 2023, https://www.history.com/topics/19th-century/ku-klux-klan.

[396] History.com Editors.

name given to a racialized social order or caste system which operated primarily, but not exclusively, in the southern and border states between 1877 to the mid-1960s. "Jim Crow was more than a series of rigid anti-black laws. It was a way of life."[397] Under the system of *Jim Crow*, African Americans were consigned to the rank of second-class citizens, as emphasized by African American Professor Emeritus, Adolph L. Reed Jr., "We were all unequal, but [when it came to race and class], some were more unequal than others."[398] Divisions amongst the lower classes, throughout the South, served as a powerful and effective hegemonic tool of supremacy. Hence, it was not long, thereafter, within that stratified class society, before that black-white alliance had ended - as Democrats slowly united in a series of successful white supremacy campaigns to banish the Fusionists and discontinue what most white southern racists denoted to as, "Negro rule."[399] Hence, as noted throughout this study, class, race, and racism have long been fundamental elements of control woven within this class-conscious slave culture, paradoxically, self-described, "birthplace of freedom."

---

[397] "What Was Jim Crow - Jim Crow Museum," accessed August 29, 2024, https://jimcrowmuseum.ferris.edu/what.htm.

[398] Adolph L. Reed, *The South: Jim Crow and Its Afterlives* (London; New York: Verso Books, 2022), 41.

[399] "What Was Jim Crow - Jim Crow Museum."

CONCLUSION

From the outset, as early as the Constitutional Convention of 1787, it has been inherently difficult to reconcile a faith in the U.S. Constitution as a "living, flexible and changeable," document - with the fundamental unfeasibility of making systemwide class transformation in the United States of America. There is copious and convincing evidence that the U.S. Constitution was intended and/or mechanized, by design, to stifle and/or inhibit any "meaningful systemic change," in order to counteract anything that does not assist the benefits of the moneyed elite. Brilliantly designed and implemented by those acclaimed early American "Framers," such as James Madison, Alexander Hamilton, John Jay, and others - the means and complex configurations woven within the U.S. Constitution were deliberately intended to be unchangeable when it came to any and all challenges from below. The Constitutional aphorism over "the rights of private property possession" and its accompanied protections for example - made possible by the "expropriation of Native Americans lands, slavery; and the exploitation of lower-class labor" as discussed – has served, from the very beginning of that early American experiment, as a primary preset to protect wealth.[400] Political Science Professor Robert Ovetz argues, in fact, that the U.S.

---

[400] Ovetz, *We the Elites*, 159.

Constitution has never really lived up to its well-known first three words, of "We the People," insisting that that renowned Charter is, by its very nature and design, "self-breaching," because "we the people have never directly given consent to be governed by it - nor do the laws put in place give [the people] the liberty to do so."[401] That said, given the complexity of mind of those men recognized as "the Framers," and in their defense, they did interweave a certain language of liberty, in the form of protections, as exemplified in Amendment IX, which states, "The enumeration in the Constitution of certain rights shall not be construed to deny or disparage others retained by the people."[402]

Amendment IX to the Constitution was authorized on December 15th, 1791. And, it clearly proclaims that the text is not a wide-ranging list of every right of the citizen, but that the unnamed rights to come will be allowed protections under the law.[403] The IX Amendment explicitly acknowledged that the people have a reserve of rights that go beyond the Constitution. Hence, the enumeration of specific rights "shall not be construed to deny or disparage others retained by the people."[404] As a counterweight to popular belief, American political scientist, author, and activist, Michael Parenti contends that, "those privileged delegates gave nothing to popular interests, rather – as with the Bill of Rights – they reluctantly made democratic concessions under the menacing threat of popular rebellion."[405] Race and class, in early America, not only substantiated that, "the wealthy are a better class of men," as James Madison proclaimed during the

---

[401] Ovetz, 161.

[402] "The Constitution of the United States."

[403] "The Constitution of the United States."

[404] "The Constitution of the United States."

[405] Parenti, *Democracy for the Few*, 50–51.

Convention[406] - but that wealth and privilege were correlated to intelligence and deserved protections. In fact, not dissimilar to present-day America, "According to the dogma [of that early elite colonial class] efforts to lessen inequality, through progressive taxation, or redistributive public spending, infringe the liberty of the rich," meaning the rich deserve their benefits and reward as such. Consequently, intelligence determines merit, and merit apportions rewards are those early American values which permeate the culture to this day. The working class, both Black and white alike, "that have been consigned to the lower reaches of society were there," as noted African American scholars Barbara and Karen Fields have demonstrated, "due to attributions of low intelligence" - demarcating clear class distinctions and divisions based on a model of superiority from early on which privileged an elite few.[407] The seeds of race supremacy and the hypocrisy of liberty, throughout America's long and difficult history, were planted by the Framers themselves, "most of whom accepted that human beings could be held as property and that Africans and Native Americans were inferior to Caucasians" in a multitude of ways[408] - as demonstrated throughout this study.

---

[406] Madison, "Notes on Debates."

[407] Fields and Fields, *Racecraft*, 278.

[408] Klarman, *The Framers' Coup*, 2016, 630–31.

BIBLIOGRAPHY

CLASS DISTINCTIONS THRU HISTORY IN REVIEW

Chapter one
Martin Luther King Jr. and the Socialist Within

Primary Sources:

Anonymous. "Suicide Letter," November 1964. Accessed November 15, 2020. Printed by the New York Times: https://www.nytimes.com/2014/11/16/magazine/what-an-uncensored-letter-to-mlk-reveals.html?_r=1&referrer=.

Clines, Francis X. "Reagan's Doubts on Dr. King Disclosed." *New York Times*, October 22, 1983. Accessed November 25, 2020. at https://search.proquest.com/docview/424807626?rfr_id=info%3Axri%2Fsid%3Aprimo.

King, Martin Luther, Jr. "Beyond Vietnam." Speech, New York, NY, April 4, 1967. Accessed November 5, 2020. The Martin Luther King Papers Project, Stanford University: https://kinginstitute.stanford.edu/king-papers/documents/beyond-vietnam.

————. "Communism's Challenge to Christianity." Sermon, Atlanta, GA, September 8, 1953. Accessed November 15, 2020. King Papers: https://kinginstitute.stanford.edu/king-papers/documents/communisms-challenge-christianity.

————. "I've Been to the Mountaintop." Speech, Memphis, Tenn., April 3, 1968. Accessed November 6, 2020. King Papers: https://kinginstitute.stanford.edu/king-papers/documents/ive-been-mountaintop-address-delivered-bishop-charles-mason-temple.

————. "Letter from a Birmingham Jail," April 16, 1963. Accessed November 14, 2020. At https://www.africa.upenn.edu/Articles_Gen/Letter_Birmingham.html.

————. "The Bravest Man I Ever Met." *Pageant*, June 1965. Accessed November 6, 2020. At https://freepress.org/article/bravest-man-i-ever-met.

————. "The Other America, Address at Local 1199." Speech, NYC, March 10, 1968. In *The Radical King*, edited by Cornel West. Beacon Press, 2015.

————. "The Other America, Address at Stanford University." Speech, April 14, 1967. Accessed November 6, 2020. At https://www.crmvet.org/docs/otheram.htm.

———. "The Violence of Desperate Men (1958)." In *The Radical King*, edited by Cornel West. Beacon Press, 2015.

———. "To Charter Our Course for the Future." Speech, Frogmore, SC, May 22, 1967. Accessed November 14, 2020. Excerpts available at https://kairoscenter.org/mlk-frogmore-staff-retreat-speech-anniversary/.

———. "To Coretta Scott," July 18, 1952. Accessed November 3, 2020. King Papers: https://kinginstitute.stanford.edu/king-papers/documents/coretta-scott.

———. "Where Do We Go From Here?" Speech, Atlanta, GA, August 16, 1967. Accessed November 6, 2020. King Papers: https://kinginstitute.stanford.edu/king-papers/documents/where-do-we-go-here-address-delivered-eleventh-annual-sclc-convention.

Reagan, Ronald. "The Creation of the Martin Luther King, Jr., National Holiday," Washington, DC, November 2, 1983. Accessed November 6, 2020. at https://millercenter.org/the-presidency/presidential-speeches/november-2-1983-speech-creation-martin-luther-king-jr-national.

"Dr. King's Error." *The New York Times*, Editorial. NYC, April 7, 1967. Accessed November 26, 2020. King Papers: https://kinginstitute.stanford.edu/sites/mlk/files/kingserror.pdf.

"FBI Special Agent in Charge, Mobile, to J. Edgar Hoover." SAC, Mobile, January 4, 1956. Accessed November 15, 2020. King Papers: http://okra.stanford.edu/transcription/document_images/Vol03Scans/96_4-Jan-1956_FBI%20Special%20Agent%20in%20Charge.pdf.

Secondary Sources:

Alridge, Derrick P. "The Limits of Master Narratives in History Textbooks: An Analysis of Representations of Martin Luther King, Jr." *Teachers College Record* 108, no. 4 (April 2006): 662–686.

Bond, Julian. "Remember the Man and the Hero, Not Just Half the Dream." *Seattle Times*, April 3, 1993. Accessed

November 5, 2020. At https://projects.seattletimes.com/mlk/archives.html#bond.

Bostdorff, Denise M., and Steven R. Goldzwig. "History, Collective Memory, and the Appropriation of Martin Luther King, Jr.: Reagan's Rhetorical Legacy." *Presidential Studies Quarterly* 35, no. 4 (December 2005): 661–690.

Boykoff, Jules. "Surveillance, Spatial Compression, and Scale: The FBI and Martin Luther King Jr." *Antipode* 39, no. 4 (September 2007): 729–756.

Bruyneel, Kevin. "The Martin Luther King Jr. Memorial and the Politics of Collective Memory." *History & Memory* Vol. 26 (April 2014): 75–108.

Hunt, Megan, Benjamin Houston, Brian Ward, and Nick Megoran. "'He Was Shot Because America Will Not Give Up on Racism': Martin Luther King Jr. and the African American Civil Rights Movement in British Schools." *Journal of American Studies* (August 20, 2020): 1–31.

Jackson, Thomas F. *From Civil Rights to Human Rights: Martin Luther King, Jr., and the Struggle for Economic Justice.* University of Pennsylvania Press, 2007.

Chapter Two
The Myth of American Exceptionalism

Pease, Donald. "American Studies after American Exceptionalism?" In *Globalizing American Studies.* University of Chicago Press, 2010.

Rodgers, Daniel T. "Exceptionalism." In *Imagined Histories: American Historians Interpret the Past,* edited by Anthony Molho and Gordon S. Wood, 21–40. Princeton, N.J: Princeton University Press, 1998.

Tyrrell, Ian, and Eric Rauchway. "The Debate Table: Eric Rauchway and Ian Tyrrell Discuss American Exceptionalism." *Modern American History* 1 (2018): 247–56.

Veysey, Laurence. "The Autonomy of American History Reconsidered." *American Quarterly* 31, no. 4 (1979): 455. https://doi.org/10.2307/2712267.

Chapter Three
The Moment King Was Slain

King, Martin Luther, Jr. "'I've Been to the Mountain Top' (1968)." Oxford African American Studies Center, September 30, 2009. https://oxfordaasc.com/view/10.1093/acref/9780195301731.001.0001/acref-9780195301731-e-33654.

————. "Martin Luther King, Jr.: All Labor Has Dignity." Truthout, January 19, 2015. https://truthout.org/articles/martin-luther-king-jr-all-labor-has-dignity/.

————. "The Other America." Civil Rights Movement Archive. Accessed October 15, 2020. https://www.crmvet.org/docs/otheram.htm.

Stanford University. "Federal Bureau of Investigation (FBI)." The Martin Luther King, Jr., Research and Education Institute, May 2, 2017. https://kinginstitute.stanford.edu/encyclopedia/federal-bureau-investigation-fbi.

————. "Lawson, James M." The Martin Luther King, Jr., Research and Education Institute, May 10, 2017. https://kinginstitute.stanford.edu/encyclopedia/lawson-james-m.

BBC4. *Martin Luther King: The Assassination Tapes*. Documentary, 2018. https://learningonscreen.ac.uk/ondemand/index.php/prog/059FE7A2?bcast=126443606.

Brown, DeNeen L. "'I Am a Man': The Ugly Memphis Sanitation Workers' Strike That Led to MLK's Assassination." *Washington Post*, February 12, 2018.

Kent, Martin. *Free at Last – Martin Luther King, Jr.* Documentary, 2018. https://www.thirteen.org/programs/thirteen-specials/free-at-last-martin-luther-king-jr-5oackj/.

Website:

Photograph by Joseph Louw: The LIFE Magazine Collection, 2005
Available at the International Center of Photography (ICP)
https://www.icp.org/browse/archive/objects/police-civil-rights-leaders-ralph-abernathy-andrew-young-jesse-jackson-and (Accessed October 4, 2020).

Chapter Four
Between Crosshairs a Man and His Revolution

Primary Sources:

Beveridge, Albert J. "Cuba and Congress." *The North American Review* 172, no. 533 (1901): 535–550.

Bonsal, Philip W. *Cuba, Castro, and the United States*. Pittsburgh: University of Pittsburgh Press, 1971.

Buchen, Philip. *Castro*. National Archives: JFK Assassination Collection, 1975. https://www.archives.gov/files/research/jfk/releases/docid-32112987.pdf.

Castro, Fidel. "History Will Absolve Me," 1953. https://www.marxists.org/history/cuba/archive/castro/1953/10/16.htm.

Daniel, Jean. "Unofficial Envoy: A Historic Report from Two Capitals." *New Republic* 149, no. 24 (December 14, 1963): 15–20.

———. "When Castro Heard the News." *New Republic* 149, no. 23 (December 7, 1963): 7–9.

Dulles, Allen. *Political Stability in Central America and The Caribbean Through 1958*. CIA: FOIA Reading Room, April 23, 1957. https://www.cia.gov/readingroom/docs/CIA-RDP79R01012A010200030001-6.pdf.

Manning, William R. *Diplomatic Correspondence of the United States: Inter-American Affairs, 1831-1860*. Washington: Carnegie Endowment for International Peace, 1932. HathiTrust Library.

"7. Memorandum From the President's Special Assistant (Schlesinger) to President Kennedy." In *Foreign Relations of the United States.* 1961-1963, Volume XII, American Republics. Washington, DC, 1961. https://history.state.gov/historicaldocuments/frus1961-63v12/d7.

"15. Summary Guidelines Paper: United States Policy Toward Latin America." In *Foreign Relations of the United States.* 1961–1963, Volume XII, American Republics. Washington, DC, 1961. https://history.state.gov/historicaldocuments/frus1961-63v12/d15.

"332. Letter From Acting Director of Central Intelligence Carter to the President's Special Assistant for National Security Affairs (Bundy)." In *Foreign Relations of the United States.* 1961–1963, Volume XI, Cuban Missile Crisis and Aftermath. Washington, DC, 1963. https://history.state.gov/historicaldocuments/frus1961-63v11/d332.

"378. Memorandum From Gordon Chase of the National Security Council Staff to the President's Special Assistant for National Security Affairs (Bundy)." In *Foreign Relations of the United States.* 1961–1963, Volume XI, Cuban Missile Crisis and Aftermath. Washington, DC, 1963. https://history.state.gov/historicaldocuments/frus1961-63v11/d378.

"Cuba: The Breaking Point." *Time,* January 13, 1961. http://content.time.com/time/subscriber/article/0,33009,828711-1,00.html.

"Cuba vs. U.S." *New York Times (1923-),* January 8, 1961. ProQuest.

"Fidel Castro's Response to President Kennedy's Speech to the Nation," October 23, 1962. LANIC: http://lanic.utexas.edu/project/castro/db/1962/19621024.html.

"Official Inside Story of the Cuba Invasion." *U.S. News & World Report,* August 13, 1979. LexisNexis Academic.

The Joint Chiefs of Staff and Efforts to Contain Castro, 1960-64. Joint Chiefs of Staff Special Historical Study, April 1981. Learn.

The Platt Amendment, May 22, 1903. https://loveman.sdsu.edu/docs/1903PlattAmendment.pdf.

Secondary Sources:

Attwood, William. *The Twilight Struggle: Tales of the Cold War.* New York: Harper & Row, 1987.

Blum, William. *Killing Hope: US Military and CIA Interventions since World War II.* London: Bloomsbury Publishing, 2014.

Borger, Julian. "Revealed: How Kennedy's Assassination Thwarted Hopes of Cuba Reconciliation." *Guardian,* November 26, 2003, sec. World news. https://www.theguardian.com/world/2003/nov/26/cuba.julian borger.

Brenner, Philip. "Cuba and the Missile Crisis." *Journal of Latin American Studies* 22, no. 1 (1990): 115–142.

———. "Kennedy and Khrushchev on Cuba: Two Stages, Three Parties." *Problems of*

Communism 41, no. Special Issue (1992): 24–27.

Chomsky, Aviva. *A History of the Cuban Revolution.* Viewpoints/puntos de vista : themes and interpretations in Latin American history. Chichester, West Sussex, U.K. ; Malden, MA: Wiley-Blackwell, 2011.

Chomsky, Noam. *Rogue States: The Rule of Force in World Affairs.* London: Pluto Press, 2000.

Chomsky, Noam, and Marvin Waterstone. *Consequences of Capitalism: Manufacturing Discontent and Resistance.* Chicago, Il: Haymarket Books, 2021.

Douglass, James W. *JFK and the Unspeakable: Why He Died and Why It Matters.* First Touchstone Edition. New York: Touchstone, 2010.

Garthoff, Raymond. *Detente and Confrontation: American-Soviet Relations from Nixon to Reagan.* Washington, D.C: Brookings Institution Press, 1985.

Hampshire College TV. *2015 • Eqbal Ahmad Lecture • Louis Perez • Wayne Smith • Hampshire College,* 2016. Accessed October 30, 2021. https://www.youtube.com/watch?v=IuBdKB8jX3I.

Kinzer, Stephen. *Overthrow: America's Century of Regime Change from Hawaii to Iraq.* New York: Times Books, 2007.

Marks, John. *The Search for the Manchurian Candidate: The CIA and Mind Control.* London: Allen Lane, 1979.

McClintock, Michael. *Instruments of Statecraft: U.S. Guerilla Warfare, Counter-Insurgency, Counter-Terrorism, 1940-1990*. 1st edition. New York: Pantheon Books, 1992.

McPherson, Alan. "Caribbean Taliban: Cuban American Terrorism in the 1970s." *Terrorism and Political Violence* 31, no. 2 (March 4, 2019): 390–409.

———. "Cuba." In *A Companion to John F. Kennedy*, edited by Marc J. Selverstone, 228–247. Hoboken: John Wiley & Sons, 2014.

Parenti, Michael. "Aggression and Propaganda against Cuba." In *Superpower Principles U.S. Terrorism against Cuba*, edited by Salim Lamrani, 65–76. Monroe, Maine: Common Courage Press, 2005.

Pérez, Louis A. "Between Meanings and Memories of 1898." *Orbis* 42, no. 4 (September 1, 1998): 501–516.

———. "Fear and Loathing of Fidel Castro: Sources of US Policy Toward Cuba." *Journal of Latin American Studies* 34, no. 2 (May 2002): 227–254.

Safford, Jeffrey J. "The Nixon-Castro Meeting of 19 April 1959." *Diplomatic History* 4, no. 4 (1980): 425–431.

Schoultz, Lars. *That Infernal Little Cuban Republic: The United States and the Cuban Revolution*. Chapel Hill: University of North Carolina Press, 2009. ProQuest Ebook Central.

Sjursen, Daniel A. *A True History of the United States: Indigenous Genocide, Racialized Slavery, Hyper-Capitalism, Militarist Imperialism, and Other Overlooked Aspects of American Exceptionalism*. Lebanon, New Hampshire: Truth to Power, an imprint of Steerforth Press, 2021.

Smith, Wayne S. "Shackled to the Past: The United States and Cuba." *Current History* 95 (1996). ProQuest.

Talbot, David. *The Devil's Chessboard: Allen Dulles, the CIA, and the Rise of America's Secret Government*. First Harper Perennial edition. New York: Harper Perennial, 2016.

Torres, Maria de los Angeles. *In the Land of Mirrors: Cuban Exile Politics in the United States*. Ann Arbor: University of Michigan Press, 2001. ProQuest Ebook Central.

Chapter Five
Better Red Than Dead

Primary Sources:

"14. George Wallace for President 1968 Campaign Brochure."
Accessed February 27, 2022. Available at:
http://www.4president.org/brochures/wallace1968brochure.ht
m.

Bureau, US Census. "Historical Apportionment Data (1910-
2020)." Census.gov. Accessed February 25, 2022.
https://www.census.gov/data/tables/time-
series/dec/apportionment-data-text.html.

Flander, Judy, and Phyllis Schlafly. "24. Interview with Phyllis
Schlafly." *Washington Star*, January 18, 1976.

Goldwater, Barry M. *09. The Conscience of a Conservative*.
Princeton University Press, 2021.

Lawrence, David. "01. America Turns the Corner." *The United
States News*, July 11, 1947.

McCarthy, Joseph R. "03. Lincoln Day Address," February 20,
1950.
http://www.historymuse.net/readings/lincolndayaddress.html.

"Platform of the States' Rights Democratic Party," August 14,
1948. The American Presidency Project - UC Santa Barbara:
https://www.presidency.ucsb.edu/documents/platform-the-
states-rights-democratic-party.

Raines, Howell. "George Wallace, Segregation Symbol, Dies at
79." *The New York Times*, September 14, 1998, sec. U.S.
https://www.nytimes.com/1998/09/14/us/george-wallace-
segregation-symbol-dies-at-79.html.

Reagan, Ronald. "12. A Time for Choosing AKA Rendezvous with
Destiny." Speech, October 27, 1964.
https://www.reaganlibrary.gov/reagans/ronald-reagan/time-
choosing-speech-october-27-1964.

"The Declaration of Constitutional Principles: The Southern
Manifesto." Congressional Record. 84th Congress Second
Session. Washington DC, March 12, 1956.
https://www.govinfo.gov/content/pkg/GPO-CRECB-1956-
pt4/pdf/GPO-CRECB-1956-pt4-3-1.pdf.

Welch, Robert. *08. The Blue Book of The John Birch Society*. Fifth Edition. San Francisco, US: Hauraki Publishing, 2015.

―――. *The Politician*. Belmont, Massachusetts, United States: Privately Printed for Robert Welch, 1963.

Secondary Sources:

Anderson, Totton J., and Eugene C. Lee. "The 1966 Election in California." *The Western Political Quarterly* 20, no. 2 (1967): 535–54.

Bjerre-Poulsen, Niels. *Right Face: Organizing the American Conservative Movement 1945-65*. Copenhagen: Museum Tusculanum Press, 2002.

Cohodas, Nadine. *Strom Thurmond and the Politics of Southern Change*. New York : Simon & Schuster, c1993.

Dixon, Marc. "Limiting Labor: Business Political Mobilization and Union Setback in the States." *Journal of Policy History* 19, no. 3 (July 2007): 313–44.

Farber, David. *The Rise and Fall of Modern American Conservatism: A Short History*. Princeton, UNITED STATES: Princeton University Press, 2010. http://ebookcentral.proquest.com/lib/ed/detail.action?docID= 1011045.

Freedman, Robert. "Uneasy Alliance: The Religious Right and the Republican Party." In *Seeking a New Majority: The Republican Party and American Politics, 1960-1980*, edited by Robert Mason and Iwan Morgan. Nashville: Vanderbilt University Press, 2013.

Fried, Richard M. "Voting Against the Hammer and Sickle: Communism as an Issue in American Politics." In *The Achievement of American Liberalism: The New Deal and Its Legacies*, edited by William Chafe. New York, NY: Columbia University Press, 2002.

Gould, Lewis L. *The Republicans: A History of the Grand Old Party*. New York: Oxford University Press, 2014.

Mason, Robert. *The Republican Party and American Politics from Hoover to Reagan*. Cambridge: Cambridge University Press, 2011.

McGirr, Lisa. *Suburban Warriors: The Origins of the New American Right*. Princeton, NJ: Princeton University Press, 2015.

Reed, Adolph. "Why Labor's Soldiering for the Democrats Is a Losing Battle." *New Labor Forum* 19, no. 3 (October 1, 2010): 9–15.

Troy, Leo. "Trade Union Membership, 1897-1962." *The Review of Economics and Statistics* 47, no. 1 (1965): 93–113.

Chapter Six
What Hollywood Communicates Through the Movie Green Book: Race, Ethnicity, National Identity, Gender, Culture and Class in 1962 America

The Film:

Farrelly, Peter, Director. *Green Book.* Dreamworks Pictures, 2018.

Vallelonga, Nick, Brian Hayes Currie, and Peter Farrelly. *Green Book* (Screenplay). Dreamworks Pictures, 2018. Accessed March 7, 2021. https://www.scriptslug.com/assets/uploads/scripts/green-book-2018.pdf.

Secondary Sources:

Cash, W. J. *The Mind of the South*. New York,: A.A. Knopf, 1941.

Cobb, James C. "Introduction." In *Away down South: A History of Southern Identity*, 1–7. Oxford University Press USA, 2005.

Crespino, Joseph. "Mississippi as Metaphor: Civil Rights, the South, and the Nation in the Historical Imagination." In *The Myth of Southern Exceptionalism*, edited by Matthew D. Lassiter, 99–120. Oxford: University Press, 2010.

Duck, Leigh Anne. "Commercial Counterhistory: Remapping the Movement in Lee Daniels' The Butler." *Journal of American studies* 52, no. 2 (2018): 418–446.

Fabregat, Eduard, and Farooq A. Kperogi. "White Norm, Black Deviation: Class, Race, and Resistance in America's 'Postracial' Media Discourse." *The Howard journal of communications* 30, no. 3 (2019): 265–283.

Fox, Lisa Ann. "Cracking the Closed Society: James W. Silver and the Civil Rights Movement in Mississippi." ProQuest Dissertations Publishing, 2010.

Hall, Michael Ra-Shon. "The Negro Traveller's Guide to a Jim Crow South: Negotiating Racialized Landscapes during a Dark Period in United States Cultural History, 1936-1967." *Postcolonial studies* 17, no. 3 (2014): 307–319.

Izzo, David Garrett, ed. "Introduction." In *Movies in the Age of Obama: The Era of Post Racial and Neo-Racist Cinema*. Lanham: Rowman & Littlefield, 2015.

Jackson, Thomas F. *From Civil Rights to Human Rights: Martin Luther King, Jr., and the Struggle for Economic Justice*. University of Pennsylvania Press, 2007.

Jansson, David R. "'A Geography of Racism': Internal Orientalism and the Construction of American National Identity in the Film *Mississippi Burning*." *National Identities* 7, no. 3 (September 1, 2005): 265–285.

———. "Internal Orientalism in America: W.J. Cash's The Mind of the South and the Spatial Construction of American National Identity." *Political Geography* 22, no. 3 (March 1, 2003): 293–316.

Johnson, Corey, and Amanda Coleman. "The Internal Other: Exploring the Dialectical Relationship Between Regional Exclusion and the Construction of National Identity." *Annals of the Association of American Geographers* 102, no. 4 (2012): 863–880.

Keeling, Kara. *The Witch's Flight the Cinematic, the Black Femme, and the Image of Common Sense*. Perverse modernities. Durham, Durham, N.C. ; London: Duke University Press, 2007.

Key, V. O., and Alexander Heard. *Southern Politics in State and Nation*. New ed. Knoxville: University of Tennessee Press, 1984.

McPherson, James M. "Antebellum Southern Exceptionalism: A New Look at an Old Question." *Civil War History* 50, no. 4 (December 2004): 418–433.

Meghana V Nayak and Christopher Malone. "American Orientalism and American Exceptionalism: A Critical Rethinking of US Hegemony." *International Studies Review* 11, no. 2 (2009): 253–276.

Pease, Donald E. *The New American Exceptionalism.* Critical American Studies series. Minneapolis: University of Minnesota Press, 2009.

Pessen, Edward. "How Different from Each Other Were the Antebellum North and South?" *The American Historical Review* 85, no. 5 (1980): 1119–1149.

Reed, Adolph L. "The Underclass Myth." In *Class Notes: Posing as Politics and Other Thoughts on the American Scene*, 93–100. New York, NY: The New Press, 2000.

Reed, Toure. *Toward Freedom: The Case Against Race Reductionism.* U.K.: Verso, 2020. Accessed February 28, 2021.

Rodgers, Daniel T. "Exceptionalism." In *Imagined Histories: American Historians Interpret the Past*, edited by Anthony Molho and Gordon S. Wood, 21–40. Princeton, N.J: Princeton University Press, 1998.

Said, Edward W. *Orientalism.* New York: Vintage Books, 1979.

Spangler, Lynn C. *Television Women from Lucy to Friends: Fifty Years of Sitcoms and Feminism.* Westport, Conn.: Praeger, 2003.

Staszak, Jean-François. "Other/Otherness." In *International Encyclopedia of Human Geography: A 12-Volume Set*, edited by Rob Kitchin and N. J. Thrift, 25–31. Second Edition. Oxford : Elsevier Science, 2009.

Terri Francis. "Whose 'Black Film' Is This? The Pragmatics and Pathos of Black Film Scholarship." *Cinema Journal* 53, no. 4 (2014): 146–150.

Theoharis, Jeanne, and Komozi Woodard. "Introduction." In *The Strange Careers of the Jim Crow North: Segregation and Struggle Outside of the South*, edited by Brian Purnell, 1–42. New York: University Press, 2019.

Veysey, Laurence. "The Autonomy of American History Reconsidered." *American Quarterly* 31, no. 4 (1979): 455.

Wilson, Ernest J III. "Orientalism: A Black Perspective." *Journal of Palestinian Studies* 10, no. 2 (1981): 59–69.

Woodward, C. Vann. "Review of The Mind of the South." *The Journal of Southern History* 7, no. 3 (1941): 400–401.

Media:

Chow, Andrew R. "What to Know About the Controversy Surrounding *Green Book*." *Time*, February 24, 2019. https://time.com/5527806/green-book-movie-controversy/.

Cieply, Michael. "Films with Black Stars Seek to Break International Barriers." *The New York Times*, February 28, 2007, sec. Movies. Accessed March 14, 2021. https://www.nytimes.com/2007/02/28/movies/28color.html.

Dargis, Manohla, and A. O. Scott. "Hollywood, Separate and Unequal." *The New York Times*, September 16, 2016, sec. Movies. Accessed February 25, 2021. https://www.nytimes.com/2016/09/18/movies/hollywood-separate-and-unequal.html.

Fleming, Mike Jr. "*Green Book*: Listen to the Real Doc Shirley and Tony Lip in Tapes That Informed Mahershala & Viggo's Performances." *Deadline*, January 25, 2019. Accessed February 26, 2021. https://web.archive.org/web/20190128105620/https://deadline.com/2019/01/green-book-tapes-doc-shirley-tony-lip-vallelonga-actual-audio-mahershala-ali-viggo-mortensen-1202541392/.

Judge, Monique. "*Green Book* Has Great Acting, a Misleading Title and Palatable Racism for White People." *The Root*, November 20, 2018. https://thegrapevine.theroot.com/green-book-has-great-acting-a-misleading-title-and-pa-1830572839.

Obie, Brooke. "How 'Green Book' And The Hollywood Machine Swallowed Donald Shirley Whole." *Shadow and Act*, December 6, 2018. Accessed March 16, 2021. https://shadowandact.com/the-real-donald-shirley-green-book-hollywood-swallowed-whole.

Russonello, Giovanni. "Who Was Don Shirley? 'Green Book' Tries to Solve the Mystery." *The New York Times*, November 2, 2018, sec. Movies. Accessed February 26, 2021. https://www.nytimes.com/2018/11/02/movies/don-shirley-green-book.html.

Scott, A. O. "'Green Book' Review: A Road Trip Through a Land of Racial Clichés." *The New York Times*, November 15, 2018, sec. Movies. https://www.nytimes.com/2018/11/15/movies/green-book-review.html.

Scott, A. O., and Manohla Dargis. "Movies in the Age of Obama." *The New York Times*, January 16, 2013, sec. Movies. Accessed March 4, 2021. https://www.nytimes.com/2013/01/20/movies/lincoln-django-unchained-and-an-obama-inflected-cinema.html.

Chapter Seven
Ideology and Hypocrisy Amid Slavery and Democracy - Strange Bedfellows from Time Immemorial

Primary Sources:

Aristotle (1935) 'Oeconomica', in G.C. Armstrong (tran.) *Aristotle in 23 Volumes*. Cambridge, MA: Harvard University Press. Available at: http://www.perseus.tufts.edu/hopper/text?doc=Perseus%3ate xt%3a1999.01.0048.

Aristotle (1944) *Politics*. Translated by H. Rackham. Cambridge, Mass: Harvard University Press (Loeb Classical Library). Available at: https://catalog.perseus.org/catalog/urn:cts:greekLit:tlg0086.tl g035.perseus-eng1.

Herodotus (2018) *The Histories of Herodotus*. Translated by A.D. Godley. Scribe Publishing. Available at: http://www.perseus.tufts.edu/hopper/text?doc=Perseus%3ate xt%3a1999.01.0126.

Homer (1998) *The Odyssey*. Translated by R. Fitzgerald. FSG Adult.

Jefferson, T. (2022) *Notes on the State of Virginia: An Annotated Edition, Notes on the State of Virginia*. Yale University Press.

Thucydides (1910) *The History of the Peloponnesian War*. Translated by R. Crawley. London: J. M. Dent -sons, ltd. Available at: http://www.perseus.tufts.edu/hopper/text?doc=Perseus%3Ate xt%3A1999.01.0200%3Abook%3D2%3Achapter%3D37.

Xenophon (1923) 'Memorabilia', in E.C. Marchant (tran.) *Xenophon in Seven Volumes*. Revised. Cambridge, MA: Harvard University Press (Xenophon, IV). Available at:

http://www.perseus.tufts.edu/hopper/text?doc=Perseus%3ate
xt%3a1999.01.0208.

Secondary Sources:

Canevaro, M. (2018) 'The Public Charge for Hubris Against Slaves: The Honour of the Victim and the Honour of the Hubristēs', *The Journal of Hellenic studies*, 138, pp. 100–126.

Canevaro, M. (2019) 'Democratic deliberation in the Athenian Assembly: procedures and behaviours towards legitimacy', *Annals HSS 73*.

Cecchet, L. (2013) 'Poverty as argument in Athenian forensic speeches', *Ktèma*, 38(1), pp. 53–66.

Cohen, E.E. (1992) *Athenian economy and society: a banking perspective*. Princeton University Press.

Hansen, M.H. (2005) *The tradition of ancient Greek democracy and its importance for modern democracy*. Copenhagen: Det Kongelige Danske Videnskabernes Selskab (Historisk-filosofiske meddelelser, 93).

Harrison, T. (2019) 'Classical Greek Ethnography and the Slave Trade', *Classical antiquity*, 38(1), pp. 36–57.

Kolchin, P. (1993) *American slavery, 1619-1877*. New York: Hill and Wang.

Lewis, D.M. (2018) *Greek slave systems in their Eastern Mediterranean context, c.800-146 BC*. First edition. Oxford, United Kingdom: Oxford University Press.

Lewis, D.M. and Canevaro, M. (2022) 'Poverty, Race, and Ethnicity', in C. Taylor (ed.) *A Cultural History of Poverty in Antiquity (500 BCE – 800 AD)*. Bloomsbury.

Morgan, E.S. (1995) *American slavery, American freedom: the ordeal of colonial Virginia*. New York: Norton.

Ober, J. (1990) *Mass and elite in democratic Athens: rhetoric, ideology and the power of the people*. Second print., with corrections. Princeton, N.J: Princeton University Press.

Ober, J. (2017) 'Inequality in Late-Classical Democratic Athens: Evidence and Models', in G.C. Bitros and N.C. Kyriazis (eds) *Democracy and an Open-Economy World Order*. Cham: Springer International Publishing, pp. 125–146.

Patterson, O. (1982) *Slavery and social death: a comparative study.* Cambridge, MA: Harvard University Press.

Rosivach, V.J. (1999) 'Enslaving "Barbaroi" and the Athenian Ideology of Slavery', *Historia: Zeitschrift für Alte Geschichte*, 48(2), pp. 129–157.

Chapter Eight
Governance, Race, Property and Profit

Primary Sources:

[Acts and Statutes] of the Island of Barbados Made and Enacted since the Reducement of the Same, unto the Authority of the Common-Wealth of England / and Set Forth the Seventh Day of September, in the Year of Our Lord God 1652 .... London: Printed by Will. Bentley, 1654.

"An Act of Regulating Servants (1681)." In *Acts of Assembly Passed in the Island of Jamaica; from 1681, to 1737, Inclusive*, 2–5. London: Printed by J. Baskett, 1738.

Aristotle. *Politics*. Translated by Harris Rackham. Loeb Classical Library. Cambridge, Mass: Harvard University Press, 1944.

Arnold, William. *Memoirs of the First Settlement of the Island of Barbados, and Other the Carribbee Islands* ... near Chancery-Lane, Holborn: E. Owen, 1743.

Engerman, Stanley L., Robert L. Paquette, and Seymour Drescher, eds. "An Act for the Better Ordering and Governing of Negroes" Barbados 1661. In *Slavery*, 105–13. Oxford: Oxford University Press, 2001.

Hall, Richard, ed. "An Act Declaring the Negro-Slave of This Island, to Be Real Estates" Barbados 1668. In *Acts, Passed in the Island of Barbados. From 1643, to 1762*, 64–65. London: printed for Richard Hall, 1764.

————, ed. "An Act for a Good Governing of Servants, and Ordering the Rights between Masters and Servants" Barbados 1661. In *Acts, Passed in the Island of Barbados. From 1643, to 1762*, 35–42. London: printed for Richard Hall, 1764.

————, ed. "An Act for the Encouragement of All Negroes and Slaves That Shall Discover Any Conspiracy" Barbados 1692. In *Acts, Passed in the Island of Barbados. From 1643, to 1762*, 129–30. London: printed for Richard Hall, 1764.

Ligon, Richard. *A True and Exact History of the Island of Barbados.* Edited by Karen Ordahl Kupperman. Indianapolis: Hackett, 2011.

Plantaganet, Beauchamp. *A Description of the Province of New Albion: Preface.* London: James Moxon, 1650.

Slavery Law & Power in Early America and the British Empire. "Jamaica Slave Code: Governing Slaves (1664)." Accessed November 15, 2023. https://slaverylawpower.org/jamaica-slave-code-governing/

Secondary Sources:

Amussen, Susan Dwyer. "Right English Government: Law and Liberty, Service and Slavery." In *Caribbean Exchanges : Slavery and the Transformation of English Society, 1640-1700.* Chapel Hill: The University of North Carolina Press, 2007.

Beckles, Hilary McD. "A 'Riotous and Unruly Lot': Irish Indentured Servants and Freemen in the English West Indies, 1644-1713." *The William and Mary Quarterly* 47, no. 4 (1990): 503–22.

Beckles, Hilary McD., and Andrew Downes. "The Economics of Transition to the Black Labor System in Barbados, 1630-1680." *The Journal of Interdisciplinary History* 18, no. 2 (1987): 225–47.

Eltis, David. "New Estimates of Exports from Barbados and Jamaica, 1665-1701." *The William and Mary Quarterly* 52, no. 4 (1995): 631–48.

Gaspar, Barry. "With a Rod of Iron: Barbados Slave Laws as a Model for Jamaica, South Carolina, and Antigua, 1661-1697." In *Crossing Boundaries: Comparative History of Black People in Diaspora*, edited by Darlene Clark Hine and Jaqueline McLeod, 343–66. Bloomington: Indiana Univ. Press, 1999.

Morgan, Jennifer L. *Laboring Women: Reproduction and Gender in New World Slavery.* Philadelphia: University of Pennsylvania Press, 2004.

Rugemer, Edward B. *Slave Law and the Politics of Resistance in the Early Atlantic World.* Cambridge, Mass.: Harvard University Press, 2018.

————. "The Development of Mastery and Race in the Comprehensive Slave Codes of the Greater Caribbean during the Seventeenth Century." *The William and Mary Quarterly* 70, no. 3 (2013): 429–58.

"The Trans-Atlantic Slave Trade Database (Voyages Data Set)." "Estimates" spreadsheet, 2023. http://www.slavevoyages.org/estimates/pUjAsKJW.

Tomlins, Christopher. "Enslaving: Facies Hippocratica." In *Freedom Bound: Law, Labor, and Civic Identity in Colonizing English America, 1580–1865*, 409–52 and 504–8. Cambridge: Cambridge University Press, 2010.

Chapter Nine
Where Negroes Are Masters (A Book-Review)

Ocobock, Paul. "Where the Negroes Are Masters: An African Port in the Era of the Slave Trade." *Canadian Journal of History* 51, no. 3 (Winter 2016): 659–61

Chapter Ten:
Philadelphia and the Darkside of Liberty

<u>Primary Sources:</u>

Aristotle. *Nicomachean Ethics*. Translated by W. D. Ross, 2009. https://classics.mit.edu/Aristotle/nicomachaen.html.

————. *Politics*. Translated by Harris Rackham. Loeb Classical Library. Cambridge, Mass: Harvard University Press, 1944. https://catalog.perseus.org/catalog/urn:cts:greekLit:tlg0086.tl g035.perseus-eng1.

Basler, Roy P., ed. *The Collected Works of Abraham Lincoln*. Vol. VII. New Brunswick, N.J.: Rutgers University Press, c1953-55.

"Declaration of Independence: A Transcription." America's Founding Documents. National Archives. Accessed March 22, 2024. https://www.archives.gov/founding-docs/declaration-transcript.

Farrand, Max, ed. *The Records of the Federal Convention of 1787*. New Haven: Yale University Press, 1911.

Foster, Augustus John. *Jeffersonian America: Notes on the United States of America, Collected in the Years 1805-6-7 and 1-12.* San Marino, Calif.: Huntington Library, 1954.

"From George Washington to Henry Knox," December 26, 1786. Founders Online. National Archives. http://founders.archives.gov/documents/Washington/04-04-02-0409.

"From George Washington to Henry Knox," February 3, 1787. Founders Online. National Archives. https://founders.archives.gov/documents/Washington/04-05-02-0006.

"From James Madison to James Monroe," October 5, 1786. Founders Online. National Archives. http://founders.archives.gov/documents/Madison/01-09-02-0054.

Hamilton, Alexander. "Final Version of the Second Report on the Further Provision Necessary for Establishing Public Credit (Report on a National Bank)," December 13, 1790. Founders Online. National Archives. http://founders.archives.gov/documents/Hamilton/01-07-02-0229-0003.

Jefferson, Thomas. *Notes on the State of Virginia.* Edited by William Harwood Peden. Chapel Hill, NC: Univ. of North Carolina Press, 1995.

Lincoln, Abraham. "The Emancipation Proclamation, 1863," January 1, 1863. https://www.archives.gov/exhibits/american_originals_iv/sect ions/nonjavatext_emancipation.html.

Locke, John. *Two Treatises on Civil Government.* London: G. Routledge and Sons, 1884.

Madison, James. "Federalist Papers: Primary Documents in American History: Federalist No. 10." Research guide. Accessed August 27, 2023. https://guides.loc.gov/federalist-papers/text-1-10.

———. "Notes on Debates," January 28, 1783. Founders Online. National Archives. https://founders.archives.gov/documents/Madison/01-06-02-0037.

———. "Rule of Representation in the Senate," June 30, 1787. Founders Online. National Archives.

https://founders.archives.gov/documents/Madison/01-10-02-0050.

Manning, William. *The Key of Liberty: The Life and Democratic Writings of William Manning, "a Laborer," 1747-1814.* Edited by Michael Merrill and Sean Wilentz. The John Harvard Library. Cambridge, Mass: Harvard University Press, 1993.

National Archives. "The Constitution of the United States." Accessed September 3, 2023. https://www.archives.gov/founding-docs/constitution.

Smith, Adam. *An Inquiry into the Nature and Causes of the Wealth of Nations.* London: G. Routledge, 1893.

"SPEECH OF FREDERICK DOUGLASS: Delivered at a Mass Meeting Held at National Hall, Philadelphia, July 6, 1863, for the Promotion of Colored Enlistments." *Liberator (1831-1865),* American Periodicals, 33, no. 30 (July 24, 1863): 118.

"Thomas Jefferson to Henri Gregoire, February 25, 1809." Correspondence, February 25, 1809. Available at: https://www.loc.gov/resource/mtj1.043_0836_0836/?st=text.

Winthrop, John. "A Modell of Christian Charity, 1630." In *Collections of the Massachusetts Historical Society,* 7:31-48. 3rd Series. Boston, 1838. https://history.hanover.edu/texts/winthmod.html.

Secondary Sources:

Baptist, Edward E. *The Half Has Never Been Told: Slavery and the Making of American Capitalism.* Paperback edition. New York: Basic Books, 2016.

Beard, Charles Austin. *An Economic Interpretation of the Constitution of the United States.* Anodos Books, 2018.

Blight, David W. *Frederick Douglass: Prophet of Freedom.* New York: Simon & Schuster, 2020.

Brent, Tarter. "Elizabeth Key (Fl. 1655-1660) Biography." In *Dictionary of Virginia Biography.* Library of Virginia, 2019. Available at: https://www.lva.virginia.gov/public/dvb/bio.asp?b=Key_Elizabeth_fl_1655-1660.

Deyle, Steven. "The Domestic Slave Trade in America: The Lifeblood of the Southern Slave System." In *The Chattel Principle: Internal Slave Trades in the Americas*, edited by Walter Johnson and Gilder Lehrman Center for the Study of Slavery, Resistance, and Abolition, 91–116. New Haven, CT: Yale University Press, 2004.

Duignan, Brian. "Enlightenment." In *Encyclopedia Britannica*, July 29, 2024. https://www.britannica.com/event/Enlightenment-European-history.

Dunbar-Ortiz, Roxanne. *Loaded: A Disarming History of the Second Amendment*. San Francisco: City Lights Books, 2017.

Fields, Karen E., and Barbara Jeanne Fields. *Racecraft: The Soul of Inequality in American Life*. London: Verso, 2014.

Finkelman, Paul. "Slavery in the United States: Person or Property." In *The Legal Understanding of Slavery: From the Historical to the Contemporary*, edited by Jean Allain, 106–34. Oxford: Oxford Univ. Press, 2012.

Foner, Eric. *The Fiery Trial: Abraham Lincoln and American Slavery*. 1st ed. New York: W. W. Norton, 2010.

Ford's Theatre. "Lincoln's Death." Accessed July 16, 2024. https://fords.org/lincolns-assassination/lincolns-death/.

Fraser, Steve, and Gary Gerstle. *Ruling America: A History of Wealth and Power in a Democracy*. Cambridge: Harvard University Press, 2009.

Gilmore, Ruth Wilson. "The Worrying State of the Anti-Prison Movement." In *Abolition Geography: Essays towards Liberation*, edited by Brenna Bhandar and Albero Toscano, 512. Brooklyn: Verso, 2022.

Gould, Stephen Jay. *The Mismeasure of Man*. New York: Norton, 1981.

History.com Editors. "Ku Klux Klan: Origin, Members & Facts." History, April 20, 2023. https://www.history.com/topics/19th-century/ku-klux-klan.

Hofstadter, Richard. *The American Political Tradition: And the Men Who Made It*. Vol Vintage Books., 1989.

Holton, Woody. *Unruly Americans and the Origins of the Constitution*. First Edition. New York: Hill and Wang, 2008.

Hubbell, John T. "Abraham Lincoln and the Recruitment of Black Soldiers." *Papers of the Abraham Lincoln Association* 2, no. 1 (1980).

Irvin, Benjamin. *Clothed in Robes of Sovereignty: The Continental Congress and the People Out of Doors*. New York: Oxford University Press, 2011.

Isenberg, Nancy G. *White Trash: The 400-Year Untold History of Class in America*. New York, New York: Penguin Books, 2017.

Kettner, James H. *The Development of American Citizenship, 1608 - 1870*. Chapel Hill, N.C: Univ. of North Carolina Press, 1984.

Kivel, Paul. *Uprooting Racism: How White People Can Work for Racial Justice*. Gabriola Islands, BC: New Society Publ, 1996.

Klarman, Michael J. *The Framers' Coup: The Making of the United States Constitution*. New York, NY: Oxford University Press, 2016.

Kohn, Richard H. *Eagle and Sword: The Federalists and the Creation of the Military Establishment in America, 1783-1802*. New York: Free Press, 1975.

Losse, Helen. "Colored Farmers' Alliance." In *Encyclopedia of North Carolina*, edited by William S. Powell. Chapel Hill, NC: The University of North Carolina Press, 2006. Available at: https://www.ncpedia.org/colored-farmers-alliance.

Lynd, Staughton. *Class Conflict, Slavery and the United States Constitution: Ten Essays*. Westport, Conn: Greenwood Pr, 1980.

McNally, David. *Blood and Money: War, Slavery, Finance, and Empire*. Chicago, Illinois: Haymarket Books, 2020.

McPherson, James M. "Who Freed the Slaves?" *Proceedings of the American Philosophical Society* 139, no. 1 (1995): 1–10.

Morgan, Edmund S. *American Slavery, American Freedom: The Ordeal of Colonial Virginia*. New York: Norton, 1995.

National Museum of African American History and Culture. "Historical Foundations of Race." Accessed July 30, 2024. https://nmaahc.si.edu/learn/talking-about-race/topics/historical-foundations-race.

Nedelsky, Jennifer. *Private Property and the Limits of American Constitutionalism: The Madisonian Framework and Its Legacy.* Chicago: Univ. of Chicago Press, 1994.

Nobles, Gregory H. "Historians Extend the Reach of the American Revolution." In *Whose American Revolution Was It? Historians Interpret the Founding*, edited by Alfred Fabian Young and Gregory H. Nobles, 135–255. New York: New York University Press, 2011.

Ovetz, Robert. *We the Elites: Why the US Constitution Serves the Few.* London: Pluto Press, 2022.

Popkin, Richard H. "The Philosophical Basis of Eighteenth-Century Racism." In *Racism in the Eighteenth Century*, edited by Harold E. Pagliaro, 245–62. Cleveland: Case Western Reserve University Press, 1973.

Reed, Adolph L. *The South: Jim Crow and Its Afterlives.* London; New York: Verso Books, 2022.

Roediger, David R. *How Race Survived US History: From Settlement and Slavery to the Eclipse of Post-Racialism.* Paperback edition. London New York: Verso, 2019.

"Timeline: Assassination of President Abraham Lincoln." In *Library of Congress.* Articles and Essays, Digital Collections. Accessed August 28, 2024. https://www.loc.gov/collections/abraham-lincoln-papers/articles-and-essays/assassination-of-president-abraham-lincoln/timeline/.

Waldstreicher, David. *Slavery's Constitution: From Revolution to Ratification.* New York: Hill and Wang, 2009.

Webb, Stephen Saunders. *1676, the End of American Independence.* New York: Knopf, 1984.

"What Was Jim Crow - Jim Crow Museum." Accessed August 29, 2024. https://jimcrowmuseum.ferris.edu/what.htm.

INDEX

Abernathy, Ralph, 17
Abolitionist Movements, 113
Adams, John Quincy, 20
African Americans, 90, 91
Africans
    Enslaved, 124, 125
    Slaves, 70, 91, 125
    Women, 121
America
    A nation of equals, 111
    Ruling class ideology, 110
    Upper-class bias, 110
American
    Capitalism, 112
    Elites, 105, 107, 120
    Exceptionalism, 12, 13, 14, 90
    Experience, 12, 88, 106
    Experiment, 131
    Freedom, 105
    Post-exceptionalist, 13
    Revolution, 87, 95
    Slave Owners, 112
    Slavery, 109
    South, 47, 48, 115
Amussen, Susan Dwyer, 75
Ancient Greek, 64, 65, 68
    Athens, 60, 62, 63, 65, 66, 67, 68
    Barbarian, 63
    City-state, 61
    Democracy, 67, 68
    Hellenic ethnicities, 66
    Identity, 57
    Poor, 67, 68
    Slave, 68
    Slavery, 68
    Thought, 57
    World, 57
Annamaboe, 80, 81
    History of, 80
Anti-Americanism, 24

Anticommunism, 35
Antislavery, 125
Anti-War Movement, 5
Appomattox, 125
Arbenz, Jacobo, 23
Aristotle, 58, 59, 60, 61, 63, 64, 67, 110, 120
    Natural slave, concept of the, 71
Articles of Confederation, 100
Atlantic Slave Trade, 78, 80
Attwood, William, 28, 29
Bacon, Francis, 88
Bacon, Nathaniel, 124, 125
Baptist, Edward E., 111, 112, 113
Barbados, 70, 77
    Act declaring the Negro-slaves of this Island, to be Real Estates (1668), 73
    Act for the Better Ordering and Governing of Negroes (1661), 72, 74
    amendments (1676), 74, 75
    Act for the encouragement of all Negroes and Slaves that shall discover any Conspiracy (1692), 73
    African slaves, 74, 78
    Atlantic World, 77
    Christians, 72
    Codified slavery, 70
    Council, 71
    Hall, Richard Esq., 72, 73
    Hawley, Henry, 71
    Irish, 76
    Jamaica

Modyford, Thomas, 77
Ligon, Richard, 71, 72, 77
Plantagenet, Beauchamp, 77
Planters, 75
Population estimates (1643-1660), 75
Race, 77
Race and religion, 72
Ruling class, 78
Slave revolt, 74
Slavery, 78
Sugar, 75
Sugar production, 71
Unfree labor, 71
White, 78
Batista, Fulgencio, 21, 22
Bay of Pigs, 23
Beard, Charles, 99, 100
Beckles, Hilary, 71, 77
Bellamy, Edward, 2
Berkeley, William, 121, 124
Beveridge, Albert J, 20
Bjerre-Poulsen, Jonas, 36, 37
Black soldiers, 116
Booth, John Wilks, 128
Borger, Julian, 29
Bork, Robert, 34
Bozell, L. Brent, 33
Brenner, Philip, 27
British
  Contracted indentured servitude, 71
  Upper classes, 71
Brown, Robert E., 15
Buckley, William F., 33, 35
Butler, Pierce, 103
Caesar, Julius, 107
Canevaro, Mirko, 67
Capitalism, 125
  American, 125
  Power of property, 101
Cash, W.J., 46, 49

The Mind of the South, 46
Castro, Fidel, 21, 22, 23, 24, 25, 27, 28, 29, 30, 31
Cecchet, Lucia, 67
Central Intelligence Agency (CIA), 23, 25, 26, 30
Chattel slavery, 68, 128
Che. see Guevara, Ernesto
Civil Rights, 5, 29
Civil Rights Act, 18, 34
Civil War, 103, 108, 113, 116, 126
Class, 88, 90
  Concepts of, 87
  Distinctions, 50, 51, 53, 67, 92, 95, 105, 133
  Relations, 128
  Unity, 129
  Working, 132
Clayton, John, 20
Cobb, James C., 46, 52
Cold War, 23, 27
Colonial Army, 96
Colored Farmers' Alliance, 116, 126, 129
Communism, 8, 24
Conservative Movement, 37
Constitutional
  Congress, 97
  Convention, 86, 95, 98, 109, 131
Continental Congress, 87, 91
Corrantee, John, 81
Counterculture, 42
Crespino, Joseph, 46, 52, 56
  Closed society metaphor, 47, 54, 56
  Mississippi
  Exceptionalism, 46
  Mississippi-Writ-Large, 47
  Mississippi-Writ-Large metaphor, 52

Cromwell, Oliver, 76, 107
Cuba, 20, 21, 23, 26, 27, 28, 30
Cuban
  Constitution, 20
  Government, 29
  Missile Crisis, 27
  Revolution, 21, 23, 31
Dallas, Texas, 29
Daniel, Jean, 28, 29
David Roediger, 117
de Crévecoeur, John, 14
Declaration of Independence, 90, 95, 125
Democratic Party, 33
Democratic Socialism, 7
Dickinson, John, 103
Dixon, Marc, 36
Douglass, Frederick, 6, 115, 116
Du Bois, W.E.B., 1
Dulles, Allen, 25
Eisenhower, Dwight D., 25, 32, 38, 39
  Administration, 21, 22
Eltis, David, 76
Emancipation of Africans, 128
Emancipation Proclamation, 113, 114, 115, 126
English, 70
  Anglo-Saxon, 119
  Capital accumulation, 75
  Colonization, 70
  Common law, 121
  Dominance, 70
  Labor institution, 70
  Magna Carta, 73
  Royal African Company, The, 75
  Suppression, 70
  Supremacy, 70

Equal Rights Amendment (ERA), 40
European, 119
  Colonists, 91
  Colonization, 118
  Constructs of race, 124
  Enlightenment, 118, 121, 122
  Enlightenment thought, 122
  Indentured servants, 91
  Superiority, 123
Fante, 81
Farber, David, 35, 41
Federal Bureau of Investigation (FBI), 8, 9
Fields, Karen and Barbara, 123, 132
Finkelman, Paul, 110
Foster, Augustus John, 106
Framers, 86, 94, 95, 96, 100, 101, 102, 131, 132
  Economic democracy, 102
  Establish Justice, 101
  Private Property, 102
Franklin, Benjamin, 91, 103
Freedom-Riders, 48
French, 70
Gilmore, Ruth Wilson, 119
Goldwater, Barry, 32, 34, 35, 38, 39, 40, 41
  The *Conscience of a Conservative*, 33
Gould, Lewis, 34
Great Society, 39
Green Book, 47, 48, 51, 55
  Ali, Mahershala, 47
  Cardellini, Linda, 49
  Carnegie Hall, 49
  Farrelly, Peter, 47, 52, 55
  Jim Crow, 48
  Kennedy, Robert F. (RFK), 53

King, Martin Luther Jr.
(MLK), 55
Mortensen, Viggo, 47
Shirley, Donald Dr., 47,
48, 49, 50, 51, 52, 53,
54, 55
African American
character, 48
*The Negro Motorist Green
Book*, 48
Vallelonga, Nick, 47
Vallelonga, Tony "Lip",
47, 48, 49, 50, 52, 53,
54, 55
character, 47
Dolores wife of, 49, 50,
55
Green, Victor Hugo, 48
Guantanamo, 28
Guevara, Ernesto, 23, 31
Hamilton, Alexander, 99,
108
Financial plan, 99
Herodotus, 65
Holton, Woody, 101
Homer, 57, 58
Hoover, J. Hedgar, 18
Hutcheson, Francis, 64
Indigenous Peoples, 90
Irvin, Benjamin, 91
Isenberg, Nancy, 90, 92, 105
Jackson, Jesse, 17
Jackson, Thomas, 4
Jansson, David R., 45, 46, 49,
54, 56
Jay, John, 120
Jefferson, Thomas, 20, 64,
90, 122, 123, 124, 125
Jim Crow, 48, 116, 126, 129
JM-WAVE, 26
John Birch Society, 37, 38
Johnson, Lyndon B., 4, 8, 18,
29, 40

Administration, 29
Great Society, 43
Judge, Monique, 53, 55
Julius Caesar, 107
Kennedy, John F. (JFK), 8,
18, 23, 26, 27, 28, 29
Administration, 25
Kennedy, Robert F. (RFK),
26
Kennedy-Khrushchev
arrangements, 27
negotiations, 27
Key, Elizabeth, 121
Key, V.O., 56
Khrushchev, Nikita, 27, 28,
29
King, Martin Luther Jr.
(MLK), 1, 2, 4, 5, 6, 16,
17, 18, 19
Abernathy, Ralph, 17
Anti-War Movement, 5
Bellamy, Edward, 2
Civil Rights, 5
Civil Rights Act, 18
Communism, 8
Democratic Socialism, 7
Douglass, Frederick, 6
Du Bois, W.E.B., 1
Ebenezer Baptist Church,
3
Federal Bureau of
Investigation (FBI), 8,
9
Hoover, J. Hedgar, 18
I've Been To The
Mountain Top, 17
Jackson, Jesse, 17
Jackson, Thomas, 4
Johnson, Lyndon B., 4, 8,
18
Kennedy, John F. (JFK),
8, 18
King, Coretta Scott, 2, 19

Lawson, James Morris, 17
Letter From a Birmingham Jail, 7
Loeb, Henry, 19
Lorraine Motel, 17
Louw, Joseph, 17
Memphis, Tennessee, 9, 10, 17, 18
Montgomery, Alabama, 8
Negro American Labor Council, 7
New Deal, 3
New York Times, 5
Nobel Peace Prize, 9
Poor People's Campaign (PPC), 5, 6, 17
Poor, Unification of the, 11
Reagan, Ronald W., 10
Reuther, Walter, 4
Riverside Church, NYC, 1
Security State, 9
Socialist, 2, 11
Southern Christian Leadership Conference (SCLC), 3, 4, 5
Stanford University, 6
Temple, Charles Mason, 18
Thomas, Norman, 2
Unification of the Poor, 18
United Auto Workers of America. *UAW*
United States, 6
Vietnam War, 1, 4, 5
Voting Rights Act, 18
War on Poverty, 4
Young, Andrew, 17
Kissinger, Henry, 30
Kivel, Paul, 118
Knox, Henry, 95, 96
Ku Klux Klan (KKK), 128, 129

Ladd, Everett, 43
Langley, Virginia, 26
Lawrence, David, 36
Lawson, James Morris, 17
Lechuga, Carlos, 28
Lewis Gould, 34
Lewis, David M., 59, 60, 62, 67
Lincoln, Abraham, 113, 114, 115, 116, 126, 127, 128
Emancipation Proclamation, 113, 114, 115
Reconstruction, 127
Locke, John, 102, 107, 108, 122, 123
Loeb, Henry, 19
Louw, Joseph, 17
Lysias, 63
Madison, James, 100, 101, 102, 105, 106, 108, 122, 132
Manning, William, 98
people out of doors, 98
The Key of Liberty, 98
Marks, John, 30
Martí, José, 24
Marx, Karl, 15
Mason, Robert, 36, 39
McCarthy, Joseph, 32, 35
McPherson, Alan, 25
Miami, Florida, 26
Military Assistance Program (MAP), 26
Mississippi, 46, 47
Monroe, James, 20
Montgomery, Alabama, 17, 51
Morgan, Edmund S., 106, 107
Morgan, Edwin, 126
Morgan, Jennifer L., 76
Morris, Gouverneur, 97

National Convention, 126
Native Americans, 91, 125
Nedelsky, Jennifer, 95
Negro American Labor Council, 7
New American Conservative Movement, 41
New Conservatism, 35, 42
New Deal, 43
New Left, 42
New York Times, 5, 22
Nixon, Richard M., 30, 42
Obama, Barack, 53
Ober, Josiah, 65
Ocobock, Paul, 81
Operation Mongoose, 26
Orientalism, 45
Orientalism, Internal, 47
Oswald, Lee Harvey, 29
Otto, Louis, 86
Ovetz, Robert, 93, 131
Ownership, 88
Parenti, Michael, 24, 86, 87, 132
Patterson, Orlando, 58, 59, 60, 63, 64, 68, 70, 75
  Slavery and Social Death, 58
Pawley, William, 25
Pease, Donald, 13
Pericles, 61, 67
  Law of Pericles, 65
Philadelphia, 85, 87, 90, 91, 93, 94, 96, 97, 108, 110
  National Hall, 115
  people out of doors, 91
Pinckney, Charles Cotesworth, 109
Plato, 61, 67
Platt Amendment, 21
Poor
  Waste people, 92
  Working, 91

Poor People's Campaign (PPC), 17
Poverty line, 4
Powell, Lewis F., 42
  Powell Memo, 42
Private Property, 102
Property, 128
Race, 65, 117, 123
  Development of, 118
  Notions of, 118
  Science, 111
  Superiority, 111, 123, 124
Racism, 111, 118, 130
Rauchway, Eric, 13
Reagan, Ronald W., 10, 38, 39, 43
  A Time for Choosing, 38
  Reagan Revolution, 43
Reed, Adolph L. Jr., 42, 51, 130
Rehnquist, William, 34
Republican Party, 37, 38, 127, 129
Reuther, Walter, 4
Revolutionary War, 98
Right-to-Work laws, 36
Robert Ovetz, 131
Rodgers, Daniel T., 12, 13, 14, 15, 45
Roman slave trade, 65
Roosevelt, Franklin D. (FDR), 3
Rosivach, Vincent, 65
Rugemer, Edward, 70, 71, 73, 78
Rutledge, John, 109
Safford, Jeffery J, 22
Said, Edward, 45
  Orientalism, 45
Schlafly, Phyllis, 40, 41
  Washington Star, 40
Schlesinger, Arthur Jr., 23, 26

Scott, A.O., 50
Security State, 9, 25
Shays, Daniel, 96
Shays' Rebellion, 96, 97, 98
Sjursen, Daniel A., 26, 27
Slave, 63, 120
    Athenian society, 62
    Labor, 112
    Society, 85
Slavery, 57, 59, 60, 70, 78,
    80, 108, 109, 114, 128
    Abolish, 103
    Abolition of, 110, 126
    Human bondage, 118
    Institution of, 114
    Institution of chattel, 126
    Study of, 81
    System of, 112
Slaves, 109
Smith, Adam, 85, 93, 104
Smith, Wayne, 25, 27
Socialist, 11
    Revolution, 31
Southern dominance, 129
Southern Manifesto, 33
Soviet Union, 28
Spanish, 70
    Atlantic World, 70
Sparks, Randy, 80, 81
    *Where the Negroes Are
    Masters*, 80
Stanton, Edwin M., 128
Susquehannock, 125
Taft, Robert, 39
Talbot, David, 23
Thomas, Norman, 2
Three-fifths clause, 102
Thucydides, 61, 67
Thurmond, Strom, 33
Trans-Atlantic Slave Trade
    Database, 76
Turner, Frederick Jackson,
    12

Tyrell, Ian, 13
U.S. Congress, 114
U.S. Constitution, 33, 85, 87,
    88, 92, 93, 95, 97, 101,
    102, 103, 108, 109, 126,
    131
    Amendment IX, 132
    Amendment XIII, 103,
        116, 127
    Amendment XIV, 127
    Bill of Rights, 88
    Centralized government,
        96
    Economic Democracy,
        102
    Fugitive Slave Clause, 110
    Preamble, 93, 102
    The Foreign Slave Trade
        Clause, 109
    Three-Fifths Clause, 109
    We the People, 93, 94, 131
U.S. News, 36
UAW, 4
Union Army, 115
United States, 1, 5, 14, 15,
    20, 28, 46
    Banking, 112
    Banks, 112
    Class biases, 100
    Foreign policy, 31
    Land of freedom, 123
    Property ownership, 103
    Race, 118
    Slave property, 112
US Strategic Air Command,
    27
Veysey, Laurence, 13
Vietnam War, 1, 4, 5, 43
Viguerie, Richard, 40, 41
Virginia, 107, 121
    Elites, 107
    Yeoman class, 107
Voting Rights Act, 18

Wadsworth, James J, 22
Waldstreicher, David, 108
Wallace, George C, 37
War on Poverty, 4
Warren, Earl (Justice), 38
Washington, George, 95, 96, 97
We the People, 43
Welch, Robert, 37, 38
    John Birch Society, 37
    The Politician, 38
Western Massachusetts, 96
Western thought, 58

White, 118, 119, 124
    Colonists, 122
    Concept of, 119
    people, 118
    Poor, 125
    Supremacy, 111
Whiteness, 118, 119
Will, George, 44
Winthrop, John, 15, 92
Worcester, Massachusetts, 96
Xenophon, 60, 62, 63, 67
Young, Andrew, 17

Made in the USA
Columbia, SC
10 January 2025

fd6a3ef1-957d-4ea1-aeb2-8a729fcc3d9eR01